Embracing GOD *in Your* SUFFERING

"If you want a book that promises you a life of instant healing and happy endings, give this book a miss. You'll be better off with the many books that specialize in empty promises. But if you want a book that is realistic about years of chronic pain and debilitating depression, yet drives you toward the comforts of Christ and his gospel, read this book. Dave Furman does not provide us with an abstract dissertation; rather, out of his own experience he shows us what it means to kiss the wave that throws you onto the Rock of Ages."

D. A. Carson, Emeritus Professor of New Testament, Trinity Evangelical Divinity School; Cofounder, The Gospel Coalition

"*Embracing God in Your Suffering* was not simply written by Dave Furman. Dave lives these words. He knows what it is to gasp for air in the churning place where wave smashes stone. With faithful endurance and Scripture-seasoned words, Dave compels us to think of our inevitable suffering theologically, not theoretically. With a courageous heart, he loves his family, serves his flock, and champions the cause of our sovereign God with a vigorous joy that belies his constant chronic pain. Jesus is the hero of his story. Dave Furman is eminently qualified to shepherd us in the matter of suffering, for not only is he a herald of God's Word, but he is also a man who is learning, over and over, to embrace God in his suffering."

Colin Buchanan, singer; songwriter

"Dave so gently reminds us that God doesn't expect us to call the hardest parts of life 'good,' but instead desires for us to hold fast to his immeasurable, neverending goodness in the midst of our suffering."

Jennie Allen, author, *Nothing to Prove*; Founder, IF:Gathering

"Dave Furman not only offers a careful exegesis of the Word of God for those who are suffering, but also shares his own story of constant pain and weakness in light of a God who loves. This is not a detached theological examination of suffering in God's world, but rather the testimony of a man who loves God and desires to live according to God's call on his life despite being unable to button his own shirt. If you're suffering, you need to read this book. If you love other sufferers, share it with them."

Elyse Fitzpatrick, author, *Home: How Heaven and the New Earth Satisfy Our Deepest Longings*

"This is a remarkable book—searingly honest, genuinely funny, relentlessly grounded, and, above all, saturated with the gospel. Dave Furman has succeeded in equipping us to face the suffering that eventually comes to all of us in a way that flows from who we are in Christ. He has provided us with a rich and moving exposition of what the Christian life looks like in real time. Let me put this simply: read this book!"

Gary Millar, Principal, Queensland Theological College, Australia; author, *Calling on the Name of the Lord* and *Now Choose Life*; coauthor, *Saving Eutychus*

"Dave Furman knows suffering and trials better than most men I know. They are not mere theoretical constructs in his life, but everyday realities that propel him into the arms of a loving Savior. With a pastor's heart and a fellow sufferer's empathy, Dave guides us with his characteristic lucidity, warmth, and clear-mindedness. He reminds us that in times of trial and trouble, far from being absent, the Father's pruning hand is closest to us. Don't read this book to merely gain knowledge or a quick fix, but to truly understand and live out the psalmist's cry, 'It is good for me that I was afflicted, that I might learn your statutes.'"

Jonathan Holmes, Executive Director, Fieldstone Counseling; Council Member, Biblical Counseling Coalition

"I was deeply encouraged by this book! It is great for anyone, but just right for someone in the midst of suffering. Few can achieve the delicate balance between biblical truth, empathy, and understanding of the struggle, while also pointing toward hope in the Lord. Dave has done this well. His meditations on Scripture comfort and encourage us to see joy in God's good plans for even the hardest trials of our life. Stories from his personal struggles and those of others add a sense of camaraderie and bring to life the fight for joy in the middle of great trials. A great resource!"

Connie Dever, author, *He Will Hold Me Fast*; Curriculum and Music Writer, The Praise Factory

Embracing GOD *in Your* SUFFERING

DAVE FURMAN

First published as *Kiss the Wave* by Crossway in 2018
This edition published in 2025

British Library Cataloguing in Publication Data
A record for this book is available from the British Library

ISBN: 978-1-783974-90-0

Designed and typeset by Pete Barnsley (CreativeHoot.com)

Evangelical Press, an imprint of 10Publishing
Unit C, Tomlinson Road, Leyland, PR25 2DY, England

www.10ofthose.com
info@10ofthose.com

1 3 5 7 10 8 6 4 2

To my sister Sarah:
you are my hero.

CONTENTS

ACKNOWLEDGMENTS

Thank you to all the saints in my life who have embraced God in their trials and pointed me to Christ in their suffering.

Gabe and Monica DeGarmeaux, I am grateful for your friendship. I'll never forget where I was standing on Capitol Hill when I received the news that tragedy had struck your family. My heart ached that day and still hurts when I remember you and pray for you. This book is what I have seen you live out every day. You have embraced God in your trials, and your faith has impacted me in a million ways. I wish I could list each one here. Thank you, dear friends.

Mary Waters, your perseverance encourages me deeply. You and your late husband, Larry, are heroes to us. Thanks for fighting for joy through headaches (literal and spiritual). You have suffered much, and yet you always look to Jesus as your comfort. Your example of lifelong ministry in the Philippines, your challenge to us to press on in seminary, your excitement for our ministry, and your support along the way have kept us going.

Ron and Kim, I admire you. You never quit. Through debilitating back pain and disability, job struggles, and children moving halfway around the world, you have continued to treasure Christ. It is no overstatement to say that my family is still overseas because of your faithful friendship to us in our trials. You have no idea how much you have inspired us in the midst of your trials, too.

Andy Domondon, your steadfast faith in pain and grief is a reminder that God does indeed work all things together for the good of those who love him and are called according to his purpose. I'll always be encouraged by your strength, which could come only from our God.

Kevin and Leslie Cathey, these last few years you have been an oasis of encouragement to our desert family in a number of ways. There have been moments filled with unknowns for us and you have helped us, prayed for us, supported us, and partnered with us in ways we would never have dreamed of. Thanks for helping us embrace God in our trials.

Sarah, I love you, Sis. You never cease to amaze me. The grace God has shown you through the darkest nights of the soul is brilliantly evident. You are gracious and forgiving, and have looked to God for solace in your pain. You have pointed me to Christ on too many occasions to count.

Redeemer Church of Dubai, thanks for your loving support. There has never been a day when I strive to care for the flock that I don't also feel cared for by the flock. You are a joy to me!

John Dyer, how could I ever write a book without your encouragement and keen eye along the way? Your friendship for over two decades has blessed me in countless ways. Thanks for first sharing the good news of the gospel with me back when we were teenagers and for pointing me to the cross every time we're together.

Darren Carlson, I suppose I should thank you for leading "the worst mission trip in the history of the world" out to our neck of the desert. Gloria and I drove through barren lands to meet you, and you introduced us to a guy who knew another guy and the rest is history. Many articles and books could be traced back to you and the bad homemade pizza we ate that day. Thanks, brother.

Andrew Wolgemuth, thanks for your partnership with our family in writing books to the glory of God. Your work behind the scenes has been nothing short of fantastic. Your representation, advice, prayer, and ninja-like editing skills should have earned your name a place on the front cover of this book. Thank you!

Jon Pentecost, your editing skills are second to none. Thanks for the hours you spent making sure I didn't say anything theologically careless or unclear. Your help was priceless.

Jonathan Holmes, thanks for reading the manuscript and uplifting my weary soul with your kind words.

Scott and Angela Zeller, it's now my second writing project where your fingerprints can be felt on every page of the manuscript. Thank you for your help, but more so for your support and friendship.

Mom and Dad, thank you for your encouragement over the years. I love you very much.

Lane and Ebeth Dennis, Josh Dennis, Justin Taylor, Dave DeWit, and Amy Kruis, thanks for your encouragement in this project.

Tara Davis, this is our second book together, and I think I can say with all honesty once again that a better editor does not exist!

I'm thankful to Jonathan Pountney, Beth Lees, and the whole team at 10Publishing and Evangelical Press for believing in this book and wanting to see it delivered to a wide readership.

Gloria, I love you, Sweetheart. This book would not have happened without you. To be honest, my life would be in shambles without you. My trials have been our trials—thanks for embracing God in them and for pointing me to Jesus.

Aliza, Norah, Judson, and Troy, I am in awe of you. Your love for me in the midst of the storms of life never ceases. Thanks for loving me on the bad days and the good days all the same. I can't believe we get to walk through life together.

INTRODUCTION

The community was abuzz as our neighbors prepared for the big religious holiday. Everyone on our street was in a good mood and extra cheerful, but I had no desire to leave our house and interact with anyone.[1]

It was difficult to go anywhere with the nerve spasms radiating through my arms. When our family left the house to run errands, my agony only intensified. We provided quite a scene for our neighbors to observe through their upstairs windows. First, my wife, Gloria, buckled our daughter into her car seat, and then she came over to the other side of the vehicle to help me. She opened my door, waited until I sat down, reached over and buckled my seat belt, closed my door, walked through the yard and opened the gate, drove the car out of the driveway, got out and closed the gate, and then returned to the car and drove us away.

Then, when we returned home, we repeated the scene in reverse. But this time, my wife carried all of the groceries—in addition to the baby—into our home. Did I mention she was also pregnant?

We came to the village intending to change the world for Jesus, but I couldn't even change my jeans without help. My nerve ailment had come back, and it was nastier than ever. I was depressed, incorrigible, and seething with anger toward God, my wife, and everyone around me.

Four months prior to our arrival in the Middle East, I'd had extensive surgery. Both my arms were operated on at the same time, and the recovery was traumatic. Years previously, I had developed a neurological disorder, lost almost all my arm strength, and suffered constant burning sensations in both arms. After a couple of years of deteriorating strength I was now disabled. I could barely use my arms. We had tried just about every other treatment option, so we were hopeful surgery would finally provide healing.

My health improved after the procedure, and my strength increased with physical therapy, so we went forward with our plans to move overseas. We were eager to start church planting work, and we hoped I would finally have the "normal," healthy body I remembered and was now dreaming of.

Then, in one moment, everything fell apart. I had dropped Gloria off at the supermarket but could not find a parking space. I drove up and down the parking lot aisles, waiting until she was done shopping. As I made a left turn, I felt a sharp burning pain in both of my arms. I instantly lost all strength. Tears flooded my face—the soreness was back. Not only had my pain returned, but it was worse than before. I lost all dexterity in my hands and developed boil-like wounds on my fingers. I couldn't stand to touch anything. I was on high-dosage medications for my nerve pain and for anxiety and depression. At one point, when I ran out of the depression medication and could not refill it in our new country, I felt like I was losing my mind. I paced up and down the length of our bedroom most nights as I yelled at myself and to myself.

I tried reading Christian books, but none of them performed the magic trick of emotional transformation I hoped for. We watched all nine seasons of a celebrated sitcom in an attempt to cheer up, but it was all to no avail.

I wanted to die.

That was almost twenty years ago. Fast forward to today, and I wish my story had a happy ending to share with you, but it doesn't. At least not the way most people describe as "happy." I am not physically healed. Although I have reasonable control over my arms and hands, I am still disabled. I can't drive, shake hands, pick up my children, open most doors, put on my seatbelt, flush the toilet, turn a key, do most household chores, change a diaper, or lift more than a couple pounds. My arms hurt all the time. I live with the burning pain from my elbows down to my forearms twenty-four hours a day. Sometimes I feel like ripping my arms off my body (though I often chuckle that I don't actually have the strength to carry out that task). I am even developing a new tingling sensation and weakness in my legs. Throughout this journey I have struggled greatly with depression, and some days life seems completely hopeless.

But something in my life did change. About two months away from starting a new church, I began to see the sun peering out from the clouds of depression. I was convicted by God for being a self-centered and hurtful husband. I also saw my own hypocrisy as a man who was about to preach to others when I was not living a life of grace myself. The most vital change was a rediscovery of God and his gospel.

All three of these things happened at about the same time, and for the first time in a couple of years the darkness started lifting. It did not totally disappear, but I saw the light of Christ once more. I again hoped in God. I began embracing my trials as something God meant for my good and his glory. I found hope again in the one God of the universe. The Lord began to teach me what the late British preacher Charles Haddon Spurgeon meant when he said that trials teach hard lessons.

Spurgeon struggled greatly with depression throughout his life and ministry. At the age of twenty-two, seven people died in a stampede during one of his sermons after someone in the crowd yelled, "Fire!" He never got over that night. He also faced intense public slander during his ministry. His wife, Susannah, was an invalid from her early thirties and could rarely attend church gatherings to hear her husband teach God's Word. Physical affliction also marked Spurgeon's own life as he struggled with intense and agonizing seasons of gout. His body ached continuously from rheumatism and inflamed kidneys. Due to these sicknesses, he was out of his church's pulpit about a third of the time, and the dark clouds of depression often hung over him. He once wrote about his depression, "My spirits were sunken so low that I could weep by the hour like a child, and yet I knew not what I wept for."[2] All this continued until God finally took him home at the age of fifty-seven.

How did Spurgeon persevere through his trials? A clue is found in a quote often attributed (though we are unsure if he ever said it) to him: "I have learned to kiss the wave that throws me against the Rock of Ages."[3] What does it mean to "kiss the wave"?

When I am in the midst of suffering, I am doing my best just to keep my head above water as the stormy waves of suffering crash over me. I have often longed to be lifted out of the rough and dark waters that feel as if they are engulfing me. I have spent many long nights despising those waves. I have never thought about embracing God in the midst of them.

I don't think Spurgeon gives us trite advice, pretending as if suffering is not difficult. I also don't think he is telling us to act as if our situations are easy: *Just try harder and kiss those waves.* No, Spurgeon tells us that God is doing more in our suffering than we can see with our eyes. None of us enjoys adversity. We want out, and yet God in his grace uses suffering for our benefit.

Spurgeon has good advice for us. Stop flailing your arms in panic and embrace the God who has sovereignly designed your circumstances. In the midst of the storm, God has your good and his glory in mind. Romans 8:28 is not just a verse for a Christian greeting card, but one we should have branded on our hearts: "And we know that for those who love God all things work together for good, for those who are called according to his purpose."

Hardship, sorrow, disability, persecution, and death are *not* good in themselves. But God in his grace uses them for our good and his glory. The nearness of God awakens us to him in our trials and draws us toward his grace. It is in these times when we need to follow Milton Vincent's counsel and stop trusting in our everchanging circumstances to bring us joy, and instead rest in the one great, permanent circumstance given to us in Christ and the gospel.[4] Jesus, God in the flesh, came to us and died on the cross, taking the ultimate wave of death and judgment upon himself so that we could be lifted up to everlasting life. Can the waves of trials drown us when we have a Savior who endured the greatest trial in our place?

The truth is, none of us is immune from suffering. If we are not currently experiencing the effects of a broken world, we will. The band R.E.M put it well when they sang, "Everybody hurts sometimes."[5] While those words may not bring us much comfort, they speak truth. Tim Keller writes:

> No matter what precautions we take, no matter how well we have put together a good life, no matter how hard we have worked to be healthy, wealthy, comfortable with friends and family, and successful with our career—something will inevitably ruin it.[6]

Maybe you're going through a great trial right now:

- You are depressed and can't see a way out of your despair.
- You are disabled, and your pain and handicap are too much to accept. You don't know if you can go on much longer.
- You had a miscarriage, and you are heartbroken that you might never have biological children.
- You were physically or sexually abused as a child and live every day in the haunting memory of what happened to you.

- You are facing weeks of chemotherapy, and you don't know if you can find the strength to make it to the hospital another day.
- You lost a loved one and miss him or her dearly.
- You hate your life. Your marriage stinks. You despise your job, and you wish everything about your life would change.

Friend, there is no guarantee that anything you can do will bring happiness or relief. No mathematical equation provides the exact roadmap or recipe to make you feel better. There is no special button to push that guarantees your life will turn around. *But* there is hope in who God is and what he has done for Christians through Christ. If you are a believer in Christ, you enjoy several realities in this present life and for eternity that are both startling and wonderful. In the pages ahead, my goal is not to give you trite advice or appeal to your emotions as a way of finding joy. We don't "feel better" by trying harder or distracting ourselves. We don't lift ourselves out of the pit through positive thinking. Instead I can think of no better way forward than to point you to the greatness of our God and all that he has done for us in Christ Jesus. It's only when we take our eyes off of ourselves and our circumstances and we gaze upon him and his work that we can keep our heads above water when the high tide of our trials comes our way. My prayer for this book is that it will lead you to the source of all hope. I pray that in your pain, you would not despair but would embrace God in the midst of your suffering.

If you feel like you can't take another day in your suffering, the Rock of Ages is with you, and he is faithful. You may not be able to embrace God in your suffering now, but this wave can take you on into a deeper, joyous walk with him.

Reading this book is not a magic formula to give you joy. But God can use these truths to lift the floodgates of your heart so his joy can fill you to overflowing.

1

LOOK TO THE SAVIOR IN THE STORM

One April evening in 2006, a group of university students and administrators were driving on a highway when a tractor trailer crossed the median, slammed into their van, killed five of the passengers, and left one seriously injured and in a coma.

It was stunning, tragic news for Whitney Cerak's family, and they were devastated upon hearing that their daughter was among those killed in the wreck. They couldn't bear to look at her body. The funeral was a closed-casket ceremony that drew well over a thousand people. Friends and family came from all over to mourn this young woman's death.

The family of Laura van Ryn, another student in the van, were thrilled that their daughter survived the crash, and they rushed to the hospital to be with her. She was in a coma, but they stood by her for weeks, praying she would wake up and talk to them once again. Then the miracle happened. Laura woke up and made some small steps to recovery that her parents documented on a website. One day Laura fed herself applesauce and played a game of Connect Four. She was becoming more alert.

But as time went on, the van Ryn family became concerned.

Some things seemed to come back to Laura, but other comments the family made didn't make much sense to her. Then one day, Laura was told to write her name on a piece of paper. To everyone's shock, the young lady in the hospital bed wrote the name "Whitney Cerak."

Laura van Ryn and Whitney Cerak looked remarkably alike. They had similar builds, facial features, and straight blond hair, and the injuries their bodies sustained in the accident made it difficult to tell the two girls apart. In the hours after the highway collision, the coroner confused the girl who had died with the one who had lived.

This scene is almost too surreal to imagine. Whitney's family had even visited with the van Ryn family at the hospital, not knowing that they were looking at their own daughter covered in IVs and tubes. They were right there in her presence, staring her in the eyes, but they didn't know it was their sweet daughter Whitney! When they finally learned the truth, they were shocked that they had been with their own daughter and not known it.

So many emotions go through my heart when I think about this incident (including deep sadness for the van Ryns). If only Whitney's family had known she was alive, they would have had peace in their distress. If only they had recognized their daughter as they stared at her in the hospital, their sadness would have turned into gladness. If only they had known it was her. It was a grave case of mistaken identity.[1]

The Disciples Didn't See Jesus

The disciples also faced a case of mistaken identity that brought them much grief. They could not grasp the identity of Jesus as the sovereign ruler of the universe. Throughout the Gospel of Mark, they don't seem to understand that Jesus is the King of the world. He is the one who holds the whole cosmos in his hands. Their failure to accurately identify Jesus leads them to fear, anxiety, and worry. In Mark 6 we see the climax of their ignorance. It was evening at the Sea of Galilee, and Jesus had just miraculously fed over five thousand people. The disciples ministered with Jesus at the feeding, but then he sent them away so he could dismiss the crowd himself. Perhaps he wanted to keep his disciples from getting swayed by the crowd's expectation of a political messiah whom they surmised would bring the promised kingdom by military force (John 6:14–15).

The Israelites had been exploited by Rome and faced heavy taxes and military oppression. As Jesus performed his miracles, messianic expectations were at an all-time high, and people began to wonder if this was the king they were waiting for. But Jesus did not come for an earthly revolution—he came for a heavenly one. He came not to kill but to die. He quickly gets his disciples away from the crowd so they don't fall prey to these political expectations. The best place to send them is on a boat across the northern part of the lake to Bethsaida. At the same time Jesus goes up on a mountain to pray (Mark 6:46).

The disciples were making their way across the sea when a storm came upon them. These professional sailors were having a rough night, soaked by the big waves and beaten down by the strong winds and darkness. Even in poor conditions the Sea of Galilee could normally be crossed during the night, but the disciples were helpless against the hard wind blowing against them.[2] Suddenly, during the fourth watch of the night (between 3 a.m. and 6 a.m.), Jesus came walking toward them on the water! By this point the men had been wrestling with the brutal storm for hours. What would the disciples expect to happen next? Jesus would save them, right? Jesus to the rescue! But what Jesus did is rather puzzling. He was walking on the water . . . and he meant to pass by them. *What?* Wasn't Jesus walking on the water in order to save the disciples? Wasn't Jesus coming to them to protect them from the storm? Relieve them from distress? Surely Jesus wasn't simply out for a midnight stroll on the lake. He wasn't trying to race the disciples to the other side. What was he doing?

The question is not whether Jesus wanted to the help the disciples. Of course he did. The better question is, *how* did Jesus want to help the disciples? What did he want to help them with? Jesus could have stopped the storm in an instant, but he was not concerned with helping the disciples make a timely arrival to Bethsaida. He wanted something bigger than that. He wanted the disciples to understand that he was (and is!) in control over the entire universe. He wanted to reveal his character to them.

The disciples could not get it. They thought he was a ghost. Over and over again in the Gospels the disciples watched Jesus perform miracles, heal the hurting, preach incredible sermons, and care for the poor—yet they failed to recognize the very Son of God. Their case of mistaken identity allowed them to entertain fearful thoughts and anxious worries. If only they had known that the man in their midst was the eternal Son of God in the flesh. If only they had known just how powerful and merciful he is—things would have been different on that stormy night on the sea.

Jesus Is the Sovereign Ruler

Jesus did indeed have a purpose in his nighttime stroll on the lake. He meant to pass by his disciples to show them he was the Son of God by explicitly pointing them back to the Old Testament. On Mount Sinai the transcendent Lord "passed before" Moses in order to reveal his name and compassion (Ex. 34:5–6). Later, on that same mountain, the Lord revealed his presence to Elijah in passing him by (1 Kings 19:11). On the Sea of Galilee Jesus was revealing himself to his disciples. They were supposed to see him and make the connection: Jesus is God.[3]

This was no illusion. Jesus literally walked on water. Job 9 says that there is an awesome separation between God and humanity. Only God can stretch out the heavens, only God can move mountains, and only God can tread on the waves of the sea. One commentator on Mark writes, "In walking on the water toward the disciples, Jesus walks where only God can walk. As in the forgiveness of sins (2:10) and in his power over nature (4:39), walking on the lake identifies Jesus unmistakably with God."[4] The act of walking on water meant Jesus is God in the flesh. There was to be no confusion about Jesus's identity.

When he "meant to pass by them," Jesus intended to make the fact of his divinity crystal clear to his disciples. And if that were not enough, Jesus yells out to his men, "Take heart; it is I. Do not be afraid." It's the exact same identification God gives when he discloses himself in Exodus 3 to Moses. Jesus takes God's name. He not only walks on water as only God can, but he also takes God's name. Jesus is telling his disciples, "I know you're going through a great trial right now, don't fear, take heart, *I am* here."[5]

The disciples let their fear overwhelm them, and it blinded them to the Savior who was right in front of them. Why didn't the disciples get it? Why were they clueless? Mark explains the diagnosis in Mark 6:52: "They did not understand about the loaves." The point of the miraculous feeding of more than five thousand people from a few loaves and fish was so that the disciples (and others present) would know that Jesus is the Bread of life, the Giver of all things. But rather than seeing Jesus as the Son of God who could provide everything they needed, the disciples failed to connect the dots. Jesus created bread from grain that never grew. He created fish that had never lived or swam or been caught by a net. He created this food out of nothing, and the crowd ate, and the people were satisfied. They ate as much as they wanted to eat. The disciples were in awe of the sheer abundance of food, but they missed the one who made the food.

I often wonder what the Twelve were thinking as they walked up and down the Galilean countryside handing out more and more bread that Jesus had made. What would be going through their minds as they came back with baskets full of leftovers? Surely they would have been stunned that Jesus had taken a few fish and a little bread and fed a crowd with more left over. However, it is easy for followers of Christ to experience the miraculous work of Christ in our midst, and then moments later doubt whether he will continue working among us. Jesus can be with us in one trial, but then at the very next one we "strain at the oars," wondering if he is going to do anything about it. I don't think we are any different from the disciples. How quickly we forget the identity of Jesus!

We will face trials and be tempted to doubt the sovereignty of Jesus. We should note that on the sea the disciples were not being scolded for being disobedient. They were doing exactly what Jesus told them to do. They were struggling with the waves because they were being obedient. The disciples were exactly where Jesus wanted them: in the middle of the angry waves of a storm. Why would a God of mercy and love and compassion do this? Precisely because he loved them so much. The disciples needed to recognize who Jesus is and to rely on him. If they understood who Jesus really is, they would be able to trust him in every storm. Jesus wanted to wake them up from the stupor of a case of mistaken identity.

We Mistake Christ's Identity

In the midst of storms in your life, have you forgotten who Jesus is? Do you doubt whether God intended for you to be in the storm-tossed boat in the first place? Do you understand about the provision of Christ himself as seen in the abundance of the loaves? Do you take courage in the fact that Jesus is who he claims to be? When you remember Jesus, does your fear vanish?

When we understand who Christ is (the sustenance-provider and storm-controller), we will have peace in the midst of life's storms. Misunderstanding who Jesus is brings us only fear and distress.

Unfortunately, we follow in the disciples' footsteps more often than we would like to admit. Our anxiety and distress are often a result of not seeing Jesus clearly. We sail through life—both on calm seas and rough waters—forgetting who commands the winds and the waves.

I do this all the time. Some days I forget the power of God, and I get so discouraged with what is happening in my life. Moments come when I feel like quitting the ministry and moving to a log cabin in the woods. Some mornings are so replete with anxiety that it takes all my determination just to swing my legs over the side of the bed and put my feet on the floor to stand up and face the day. Sometimes my arm pain is so bad I scream in agony. When I had double-arm surgery, I literally couldn't move either of my arms. At that same time we received discouraging news from some friends, and I felt utterly hopeless. I felt unable to change anything in my life (indeed, I was powerless!), and yet I was responding as if God were not in charge over every aspect in my life. James writes in his epistle:

> Come now, you who say, "Today or tomorrow we will go into such and such a town and spend a year there and trade and make a profit"—yet you do not know what tomorrow will bring. What is your life? For you are a mist that appears for a little time and then vanishes. Instead you ought to say, "If the Lord wills, we will live and do this or that." As it is, you boast in your arrogance. All such boasting is evil. (James 4:13–17)

It has always been God himself who dictates whether we live or die tomorrow. We do not know what tomorrow holds for us, but he does. Friend, our lives may be a mist, but it's a mist that God holds in his hands. It's a mist he knows about and is in control of. Isn't that reassuring? You are not an accident. Your hardship is not out of his control. God oversees your life.

It is easy to go about our days as functional atheists. We believe in Jesus but we live like he does not exist. We go through our days and face our storms forgetting Jesus and what he has done for us. The disciples' trial on the sea and your trials right now are gifts of grace. You may not think it in the depths of your pain, but your suffering can be a gift. How can this be? Our view of God's ways is like looking at the ocean from the beach: there's more of the ocean that you do not see than what you do see.[6] Likewise, there is more to your trial than meets the eye, but it is hard to remember that when we misunderstand or misbelieve who Jesus is.

One of the best things you can do when you mistake Christ's identity is meditate on truths from Scripture that describe Jesus as the sovereign ruler of the universe. Consider:

> Yours, O Lord, is the greatness and the power and the glory and the victory and the majesty, for all that is in the heavens and in the earth is yours. Yours is the kingdom, O Lord, and you are exalted as head above all. Both riches and honor come from you, and you rule over all. In your hand are power and might, and in your hand it is to make great and to give strength to all. (1 Chron. 29:11–12)

> I know that you can do all things, and that no purpose of yours can be thwarted. (Job 42:2)

> The Lord has established his throne in the heavens, and his kingdom rules over all. (Ps. 103:19)

> Our God is in the heavens; he does all that he pleases. (Ps. 115:3)

> And Jesus came and said to them, "All authority in heaven and on earth has been given to me." (Matt. 28:18)

> In him we have obtained an inheritance, having been predestined according to the purpose of him who works all things according to the counsel of his will. (Eph. 1:11)

When we know the truth of these verses, we know that our pain is not an accident. God is in control over every swell of the waves. He is sovereign over every gust of wind. The answer to our fear, stress, pain, and trials is not to merely get to the other side of the sea, but to guard against mistaking Christ's identity in the midst of the storm.

Whitney Cerak was there, in front of her family, the whole time. They looked at her but could not see who she was, and they mistook her for someone else. You must know that Jesus is the sovereign King of the universe who loves you, cares for you, and is in control over your life, or you will mistake him for someone else: a weak, helpless god. To experience peace in the midst of life's trials, we need to know Jesus is the Son of God, and we need to live accordingly. We need to consistently be reminded that Jesus is in control. Remind yourself of his power as you regularly read his Word. As you reflect on your life, remember all that God has already done for you. Even as I continue to struggle in my disability, I am encouraged as I reflect on God's comfort in the sorrow. He has cared for me on the dark nights. He has given me sweet friends who have supported me when surgeries have failed. I have a wonderful wife who never complained as she drove me to dozens of doctor appointments and physical therapy sessions and prayed hope-filled prayers as we kept asking God for healing. God has also blessed me with a church that loves deeply and has never grumbled about a "weak" pastor leading the flock. Looking at God's grace in my life has been a lifesaver. Remembering the loaves and fish of your life will help you face the storms and the waves when they inevitably arise out of this fallen world.

The waves may loom large in your life, but don't miss the loving and sovereign God who sent the storm and holds you fast in the middle of it. God is not powerless to stop the wave or to protect you in the wave. He is a good and gracious God who loves you and cares for you. This truth of God's loving control over my life has been a balm to my weary soul on numerous occasions. It's a truth that can uplift all of us when we go through trials.

2

HE IS OUR REFUGE

Here we go again.

As I write, I'm sitting in Delhi, India, a couple of days after one of the most devastating experiences of my life.

My friend Scott and I came to the city to teach a seminary class on evangelism and discipleship, and we had a delightful group of students. They seemed encouraged and had some of their paradigms for life and ministry transformed by the gospel.

We also enjoyed preaching in various churches and meeting faithful pastors. And, of course, the food was world-class! The chilli paneer I ate this week was the best I have ever had, and we found a restaurant that was so good, we went back three times. Our storytelling Sikh driver, Balbir, drove us to the Taj Mahal and one of the biggest Sikh temples in the city. Thousands of worshipers gathered early in the morning not only for worship, but to make the community meal. I had never before seen so many cucumbers and potatoes. There was even a chapati machine that would shoot out a hot chapati bread every second. It was unbelievable!

But things changed in an instant.

Scott and I decided to jump into a taxi and go out to eat in the center of the city. We ran across the street, dodging cars, autorickshaws, motorbikes, bicycles, the occasional man with a wheel barrow, and even a renegade cow. But just as I reached the taxi, I fell into a two-foot hole in the ground. Falling forward, my full weight landed on my left hand and right elbow. The pain was excruciating. I quickly stood up and began running across the side street, in shock at the nerve spasms. Because of my disability, when a nerve is struck, the only thing I can do is run in agony. Scott remarked that he was thankful I didn't run into the middle of the road, or I would have been crushed by a rickshaw. I'm thankful, too!

I've fallen a few times before, but I'd never before fallen directly on one of my elbows, the most tender and painful part of my arm. My worst nightmare happened.

Needless to say, there was no good Indian food for us that night. We went back to the hotel room, and I ordered a pizza that was hardly better than the microwave variety and lay in my bed in despair. All I could think about was that I would probably have intensified pain for days or even weeks. Perhaps my fall had caused further disability and permanent pain that would never go away this side of heaven.

Trouble Will Come

How could the most horrendous accident I had ever experienced carry me closer to the Rock of Ages? The first place I turned in my Bible in the aftermath of the accident was Psalm 46. I go back to this psalm time and time again:

> God is our refuge and strength, a very present help in trouble. Therefore we will not fear though the earth gives way, though the mountains be moved into the heart of the sea, though its waters roar and foam, though the mountains tremble at its swelling. (Ps. 46:1–3)

Notice that the psalmist presumes there will be trouble. We won't have easy lives and—at some point—we will all have difficulty. It has been said, "If you live long enough, you too will suffer."[1] It's certain. The psalmist wrote the truth that the earth will give way and the mountains, the most solid thing on earth, will not be able to withstand this fallen world. For all our science, we are still vulnerable to tornadoes, waves, and earthquakes. We can send rockets to the moon, yet the tiniest bacteria can kill us. We have no power to change the weather or the doctor's diagnosis of a fatal illness. We are helpless.

In this fallen world, pain and suffering will come. We need help.

God Is All-Powerful and Protects His People

We may trip over a hole in the ground, develop a chronic illness, or struggle with depression, but our God is the one who protects. We hope not in the things of this world, but in God himself. The psalmist proclaims this in verse 1 of Psalm 46: "God is our refuge and strength, a very present help in trouble." Therefore we should not fear. Regardless of what might be happening around us, we have God's protective presence. God is not only sovereign over all things, but he is *present*, right there with us in the midst of all things.

We are not certain of the exact historical setting of this psalm, but some suggest it may describe Jerusalem during the invasion of Sennacherib in 701 BC. During that invasion, the Assyrian king taunted the king of Israel, Hezekiah, and said that his god was better than Hezekiah's God. Isaiah told King Hezekiah that this was nonsense and encouraged him to ask God for his protection. In response to Isaiah's reassuring words, the king prayed to God, who alone rules over the kingdoms of the earth (2 Kings 19:14–19). And do you know what God did? God sent an angel of the Lord, and 185,000 Assyrians were destroyed in one night. Sennacherib was murdered by his sons and replaced on the throne.

As he did for Hezekiah and the Israelites, God can deliver his people with his very word. *In an instant.* Consider my favorite verse in this psalm: "The nations rage, the kingdoms totter; he utters his voice, the earth melts" (Ps. 46:6). The God who commands creation with his voice comes to the aid of his people with that same voice. The Lord speaks and the earth melts. It just melts. He is in complete and sovereign control.

Daniel understood this when he said: "All the inhabitants of the earth are accounted as nothing, and he does according to his will among the host of heaven and among the inhabitants of the earth; and none can stay his hand or say to him, 'What have you done?'" (Dan. 4:35).

Paul says in Colossians 1:

> For by him all things were created, in heaven and on earth, visible and invisible, whether thrones or dominions or rulers or authorities—all things were created through him and for him. And he is before all things, and in him all things hold together. (Col. 1:16–17)

Here is the comfort: This God who can melt the earth with his voice is *with* us: "The LORD of hosts is with us; the God of Jacob is our fortress" (Ps. 46:7). And this refrain is repeated in verse 11.

"Hosts" is a military term that means armies. The Lord of all armies is with us. His protective presence is described as a fortress: an isolated, elevated stronghold against an enemy. It—*he*—is a safe place of protection.

What made Jerusalem special was not the temple itself or the city's heritage. It was the presence of God. The living God dwelt there. The point is this: God is a sufficient defense. He is our only defense. His presence and power cast out all our fears. Spurgeon used to say, "We are slow to meet him but he is never tardy to help us."[2] God is our refuge.

This idea of refuge would have instantly reminded the Israelites of the cities of refuge that were throughout their land (Num. 35:9–11). These cities were designated as safe cities. In those days, justice worked on the principle of an "eye for an eye" or a "tooth for a tooth." If you hurt anybody—even by accident—you'd better watch out for justice.

The cities of refuge were a picture of mercy. If a man killed somebody by accident, he could flee to one of these cities without fear of reprisal. So, for instance, if you accidentally killed a man by a mechanical malfunction on the job, the thing to do was to immediately flee to the closest City of Refuge. The goal was to get yourself through the gates of the city before you got caught. You would spend the rest of your life in that city, but at least you were safe from revenge.

God was not a refuge only for accidental offenses back in Levitical times. He is our refuge always. The point is, when the earthquake hits or the storm approaches or discouragement engulfs or war breaks out in the streets in front of your house or in the confines of your heart, don't ignore it and don't fight it yourself. Head for the ultimate City of Refuge. Admit you have no hope on your own, and head to God, our refuge and protection.

Jesus said, "Come to me, all who labor and are heavy laden, and I will give you rest" (Matt. 11:28). God is with us. He is continually available. He is an ever-present help and can be found whenever we need him.

Picture the following:

> There is a river whose streams make glad the city of God, the holy habitation of the Most High. God is in the midst of her; she shall not be moved; God will help her when morning dawns. (Ps. 46:4–5)

This river is placid in contrast to the raging waters of the previous verses. Rather than destruction, this river offers rejoicing.

God's presence is like a refreshing river flowing through the city. Cities often develop alongside rivers because rivers offer life. If you look at old pictures of Dubai (the city I live in), you will see that the city could be found on both sides of Dubai Creek (which is more like a large river) and grew out from there. The creek brings food and trade. The psalmist says that God is in the midst of us, like a river bringing life, gladness, and joy. God's protective presence not only keeps us from harm's way but also brings us all we need. God keeps us both safe and satisfied.

Trust in This God

All of Psalm 46 builds to the command in verse 10. In the imperative, we hear God breaking into the scene in the first person: "Be still, and know that I am God. I will be exalted among the nations, I will be exalted in the earth!"

God is not making a suggestion or an encouragement. This is a command. It has the force of a military order. Cease! Desist! Attention! It's not merely, "Shh . . . could you be quiet?" God is insistent. It's tough to see the force of this imperative in English, but God is speaking to us like a parent separating two fighting children. Stop it! Pay attention! Calm down and be still! Stop running around looking to other gods! God is telling us to stop worrying about life. To stop being afraid. To pause for a minute and be still and know that he is God.

This knowing isn't merely intellectual. Knowing God is not less than factual knowledge but it is more than factual knowledge. You can know that there is "God" but not actually *know* this God.

James tells us that even the demons in hell know that there is one God, and shudder (James 2:19). But the "knowing" in Psalm 46 is much more than that. This kind of knowing is a knowledge of observation *and* affection. We must see and savor God. For the believer, by the Holy Spirit we are able to see and to love what we see. Our eyes are opened to not only know God but to delight in him.

That's the difference between the demons and us. Only by looking at *and* loving him can he become our refuge, strength, and fortress.

This command may be exactly what you need to hear God say to you today. Stop, pay attention, be still and know—at a heart level— that I am God. This passage reminds us of

Jesus's statements in the Sermon on the Mount: "Therefore I tell you, do not be anxious about your life, what you will eat or what you will drink, nor about your body, what you will put on. Is not life more than food, and the body more than clothing?" (Matt. 6:25).

Jesus is saying don't worry even if these things are lacking. Don't worry even if you are dying of hunger, thirst, or exposure. Don't fear even if the world disintegrates around you, for our refuge remains secure.

God Is Never Shaken

Elisabeth Elliot lived a life full of earth-shattering events. The first was when her husband Jim Elliot was killed by Auca Indians in Ecuador while trying to reach them with the gospel. Five young men flew into the jungle to take the gospel to a violent tribe, and they were all speared to death within minutes of landing their plane. Years later, her second husband, Addison Leitch, was slowly consumed by cancer in a devastating manner. In describing what these experiences were like, Elisabeth referred to Psalm 46:

> In the first shock of death everything that had seemed most dependable had given way. Mountains were falling, the earth was reeling. In such a time it is a profound comfort to know that although all things seem to be shaken, one thing is not: God is not shaken . . . the thing that is most important is to do what the psalmist does later, to be "still" and know that God is God. God is God whether we recognize it or not. But it comforts us and infuses strength into our faltering spirits to rest on that truth.[3]

That is the point of the psalm. There will be trouble, but God offers a loving presence as a refuge. Our call is to trust him. To be still and know that he is God. Friend, we must understand that even in the midst of utter chaos, God is with us. He is *with* us and he is *for* us.

Unless we understand that with our hearts, we will be afraid.

If God is your treasure, your soul will never be empty.

If God is your refuge, you will never be deserted.

If God is your fortress, you will never be unprotected.

Jesus bore the full wrath of the Father to bring the ultimate war to an end. Go to him today. Trust in God.

The God of Psalm 46 commands angelic hosts, volatile nature, expanding creation, historical chaos, wars, and rumors of wars. He is the Lord of hosts. No wonder then that this psalm inspired Martin Luther's great hymn, "A Mighty Fortress Is Our God." During tough moments in the Reformation, he and his good friend Philip Melanchthon would sing it together as a reminder of God's unfailing faithfulness to protect his people from ultimate danger. May we too find deep encouragement.

God Is Your Refuge

A man who attended our church on occasion understands well that our God is a God of protection. He is from a country where Christianity is forbidden, and on Christmas a number of years ago the police arrested dozens of church leaders in his country. Men and women were dragged out of their homes without warning. My friend was separated from his wife and two children and arrested. He spent six years in prison. During his stay there, he wrote a letter to his father. Years ago, I was able to obtain an excerpt from that letter.

Dear Dad,

Please accept my warmest greetings from the heart of prison in the name of Jesus. . . .

I have gone through difficult days, but more than ever before I have seen myself in the bosom of the Lord, which is full of love. I have had a deep experience of loneliness, but I have never felt alone.

Often I have been sorrowful because of certain things, but I have never been a slave of sadness. Often I have been insulted, humiliated and accused, but I have never doubted my identity in Christ. Some have deserted me, some have fled from me . . . but my Lord has never left me.

I spent 361 days in a locked cell, and I did not see the sunlight for days, but the mercies of the Lord were made new every morning. I have many things to say, but I like to say how much I love you. I miss you. . . .

Probably I cannot be with you for a few years. However your word and exhortations are in the ear of my soul. I hope that at the end I will be able to see you. But if the Father calls me to the eternal abode, please protect and support my family more than before, especially my children who are dearest of my heart.

The narrow way, that I am passing through I see as a cup that my Beloved has given me, and I will drink it to the end, whatever that end might be. What really matters is that I am my Beloved's and my Beloved is mine. This possibly is the sweetest truth of my life that I am His and He is mine. . . .

The flock is cut off from the fold. Yet we rejoice in the Lord and take joy in the God of our salvation. Because neither the walls nor the barbed wires, nor the prison, nor suffering, nor loneliness, nor enemies, nor pain, nor even death separates us from the Lord and each other.

With love and greetings in Christ.

My brother in Christ understood that God is his refuge. He understood that "the nations rage, the kingdoms totter; he utters his voice, the earth melts. The Lord of hosts is with us; the God of Jacob is our fortress. . . . 'Be still, and know that I am God. I will be exalted among the nations, I will be exalted in the earth!'" (Ps. 46:6–7, 10).

Some of us will find ourselves suffering not from a physical imprisonment but from a spiritual one—or from an emotional one as we battle depression. I think of a friend in the ICU about to face the imprisonment of chemotherapy sessions and quarantine from his children. For me, my arms still hurt. I'm discouraged. I fell into a hole on my trip to India. But God was not surprised by the hole. That "tidal wave" that crashed upon me on the street was not an accident. He is a God who cares for me and provides refuge for me in his loving care. He is drawing me nearer to the Rock of Ages. I see that more clearly now.

3

THE ULTIMATE RESCUE MISSION

On Christmas Eve 2012, Martin and Maria and their two daughters came to our church's worship gathering for the first time. This family, from a restricted-access country nearby, had never stepped foot into a Christian meeting of any kind. But something drew them when some of our church members invited the family to celebrate Christmas at our special Christmas Eve service. As many churches throughout the world do, every year on this night we gather to read passages about the birth of Jesus, sing Christ-centered Christmas carols, and hear a short devotional. It is a festive night, and many of our friends, coworkers, and neighbors join us. We pray for this event all year, hopeful that many lives will be changed as people hear the good news of the gospel.

As they related to us later, during the presentation of the gospel that year both Martin and Maria felt a warm sensation come over their bodies that they had never felt before. They had not heard that God came to earth to save people from their sins. The message of Christmas stuck in their minds, and they wanted to hear more about this God who would send his Son to earth to save his people.

They were stunned.

In the same way, Christians should never get over the incarnation of Jesus. It's surprising that God would come to us. When we are walking through trials of various kinds, we need to remember this truth. God did not leave us alone in this world. The Son of God left heaven and came to earth. He faced incredible pain and suffering himself to rescue us from our sin and bring us hope in our trials.

The Epic Birth Announcement

Parents often send out a birth announcement with a picture of their newborn and various details about their baby. These announcements might include a photo, the date and time of birth, height and weight of the child, and the name. If Jesus had a birth announcement, it would be out of this world. For the date, it would say "from eternity past" (maybe with a clarification that his human incarnation had just happened). To describe his name it would say that Jesus means "the one who saves." But his height and weight would look like any other baby, since he really was born like everyone else. He was fully man and fully God. His mother Mary's conception and pregnancy were miraculous. God the Holy Spirit put the baby in the virgin Mary's womb.

In truth, Jesus did have a birth announcement, though it was unlike anything seen before in history. An angel made the announcement to a group of shepherds:

> And in the same region there were shepherds out in the field, keeping watch over their flock by night. And

> an angel of the Lord appeared to them, and the glory of the Lord shone around them, and they were filled with great fear. And the angel said to them, "Fear not, for behold, I bring you good news of great joy that will be for all the people. For unto you is born this day in the city of David a Savior, who is Christ the Lord." (Luke 2:8–11)

This was an epic birth announcement. But this announcement was not simply that a baby was born, but that this baby was good news for all people because this baby was Christ the Lord. The Savior of the world had come!

This was the birth that all of history had pointed to. Since the creation and subsequent fall of the first two humans, all of creation had been groaning and waiting for redemption (and still is). Adam and Eve were made to be in fellowship with God, but they rebelled against God and rejected his loving rule. Like our first parents, we all, by nature, want to live our lives apart from God. The Bible is clear that sin against a holy and perfect God can lead only to death and judgment. The rest of the Old Testament, after we learn about Adam and Eve, is the story of God's promise to rescue sinners. We first read about the promised Rescuer in Genesis 3:15. Later, God reiterates this promise to Abraham, telling him that the Rescuer would come through his line. Generations later, God told David that a greater King would come from his biological line. And prophet after prophet called God's people to repentance, describing the work the Rescuer would do in delivering them and in judging those who reject God's rule. And now, after all those years, the promised Savior was born.

Hurting friend, this truth means everything to us while we struggle in our trials. There is hope.

A Birth Story to Remember Again and Again

My kids love hearing the stories of when they were born. No matter how many times they've heard it before, they want us to repeat their birth story with the same details over and over again. For instance, we tell our oldest, Aliza, that Daddy had to leave an amazing dinner at church and blitz through traffic like a race car driver. I tell her that when I arrived home to take Mommy to the hospital, I actually ate some leftover brisket tacos first (don't judge me!). And then as we were taking her home from the hospital two days later on Easter weekend, snowflakes actually fell out of the sky in Dallas! She loves to hear the story again and again.

In a similar way, we remember the story of Jesus's birth because it brings joy to our hearts. When babies are born, they change their parents' lives forever. But when Jesus was born, he didn't simply change the daily life of one couple; he was born to be the center of the entire universe. Hurting Christian, this birth story means that God came for you. Colossians 2:9 says, "For in [Christ] the whole fullness of deity dwells bodily." Jesus is God-in-the-flesh. God had come to dwell among his people. D. A. Carson puts it this way:

> This Word became something he wasn't. He already existed; he was God's own agent in creation, but now he becomes a human being. And this human being is Jesus. John's Gospel does not tell us that the Word merely clothed himself in animal humanity, or pretended to be human, or coexisted with a man

> called Jesus. Nor does it imagine that all of God is exhausted in Jesus (for then Jesus would not have had a heavenly Father to whom to pray!). The language is exquisitely precise: the Word became flesh; the Word, without ceasing to be the Word, became a human being . . . God and man.[1]

God became man without ceasing to be God. As miraculous as this sounds (and it is!), this is what had to happen to save us from our sin. God had to come be with us. Remembering the incarnation is a startling reminder of the depth of the gospel. Michael Reeves says, "The virgin birth is an almighty 'No!' to all our silly attempts at earning salvation. . . . In his birth of a virgin he was not giving us an example; he was becoming our Savior."[2] The virgin birth alerts us to the miraculous intervention of God to save us from our sins. Christ took our flesh and blood in order to heal us of our sins. Hebrews 2:14 says, "Since therefore the children share in flesh and blood, [Jesus] himself likewise partook of the same things, that through death he might destroy the one who has the power of death, that is, the devil."

Christmas is not a stand-alone event in salvation history. It is connected to Good Friday and Easter. Jesus, the Son of God, left heaven in order to redeem us. Christ's birth was the ultimate rescue mission. For everyone else it would have been mission impossible. But for him and only him it was possible to be both God and man. We must not forget the depth of this rescue mission. On our own we had no hope of raising our dead souls and bodies to new life. But he left heaven and was born of a woman so that we could be born again to new life and one day live with him in the new heavens and new earth. In our heartbreak and sorrow, we have hope that God has entered into our world to rescue us from our sin. Dwell on that truth for the rest of your life.

He Understands Our Pain

Many people may have tried to comfort you in your suffering by saying things like, "I know exactly how you feel" or "Your grief reminds me of a time when I went through something." But unless they're Jesus, it's almost never helpful for someone to say to us they know exactly how we feel when we are going through a trial. Jesus, however, could say it because he is all-knowing and does know what you are going through. Furthermore, he did not simply put on our clothes as a man; he put on our flesh.

Jesus faced all the pain and disappointment of life as a human being. He knows how it feels to be tempted and to suffer loss. Jesus knows what it is like to cry tears, to feel betrayed. He was rejected by those close to him, and he felt physical affliction. He was ignored by his friends, and he tasted death. Jesus identifies with us in every way. He faced torment at the greatest level when he was forsaken by God the Father at the cross, crushed by the wrath of God and the weight of our sins.

Even in our worst trials, when the waves are crashing upon us, we can say in faith: "Jesus, you understand. You understand what I am going through." And he does. He understands what it's like to be a teenager. He understands what it's like to have shooting nerve pain in his body. He knows what it's like to be poor, to be mocked, beaten, and abused. He knows what it's like to be betrayed by a friend. He knows what it's like to face trials as an innocent one. He knows.

He understands our pain. How comforting that he "gets" us. Here is what the book of Hebrews has to say about this:

> Since then we have a great high priest who has passed through the heavens, Jesus, the Son of God, let us hold fast our confession. For we do not have a high priest who is unable to sympathize with our weaknesses, but one who in every respect has been tempted as we are, yet without sin. Let us then with confidence draw near to the throne of grace, that we may receive mercy and find grace to help in time of need. (Heb. 4:14–16)

He is our High Priest who can identify with us in every way.

In ancient Israel the priest represented the people to the Lord by offering sacrifices at the tabernacle or temple. On the Day of Atonement, the high priest would go into the Most Holy Place and offer the annual sacrifice for himself and the people. Since the high priest was a man and tempted like everyone else, he could represent the people before God. Jesus is not only the one who as our representative saves us; he is also the perfect one who can fully relate to us and anything we're going through.

Whatever trial you are walking through, Jesus has been through it. This is so helpful for me to remember when I face my physical pain. Any mild persecution I might encounter in our ministry here in the Middle East pales in comparison to what Jesus faced when he was mocked and killed. As one prone to depression, I find comfort in remembering that Jesus went through the most depressing state possible: being separated from God the Father on the cross. When the nerve damage in my arms is unbearable, I think about the nails that pierced Jesus's arms right through the nerves. When I go through difficult family circumstances, I recall that Jesus's family didn't believe he was Lord. When I miss my friends who live half the world away from me, I remember that Jesus left his throne in heaven to come to earth. When money is tight, I remember that Jesus was poor and didn't own more than the clothes he wore. When I am facing endless temptation, I know Jesus can sympathize with my weaknesses because he was tempted just like we are.

Friend, Jesus knows.

Jesus Left, but He Left Us with the Spirit

Though Jesus doesn't walk on the earth today, we remember that when he left the earth in his ascension, he didn't really leave us. In fact, he told his disciples that it was better that he depart: "Nevertheless, I tell you the truth: it is to your advantage that I go away, for if I do not go away, the Helper will not come to you. But if I go, I will send him to you" (John 16:7).

God came to earth in the incarnation, and he sent the Spirit of God to remain with us. Christian, the Spirit of God dwells in you! There is no more tabernacle. There is no more temple. As believers, *we* are the tabernacle. *We* are the temple. God's Spirit dwells within *us*, his church. Paul said to the Corinthians, "Do you not know that you are God's temple and that God's Spirit dwells in you?" (1 Cor. 3:16). Jesus said to his disciples, "I will ask the Father, and he will give you another Helper, to be with you forever, even the Spirit of truth, whom the world cannot receive, because it neither sees him nor knows him. You know him, for he dwells with you and will be in you" (John 14:16–17).

Fellow Christian, God is with you. Literally. When you feel alone, he is with you. When you grieve, he grieves. When you are hurting, he is there to comfort you. When you don't know what to do, the Spirit of God will give you direction. When you don't know what to pray, he will help you with groanings too deep for words. The indwelling of the Holy Spirit has profound implication on all areas of our lives. It is no trite platitude that God came for his people and remains with them. It is a cosmic-altering reality.

This truth of God coming to us so delighted Martin and Maria that Christmas Eve that they could not get Jesus out of their minds. Over the next four months they studied the Bible with the friends who had brought them to our worship service. Soon they could see that Jesus is Lord over all. They understood that Jesus came to earth to die for their sins. Both of them repented of their sin and trusted in Christ to save them. They were baptized in our church, and soon Martin helped lead a small group of people from his nation with the hopes of one day seeing it become a church.

Martin and Maria continue to cling to this truth that God came to save them. They have faced trial and persecution, but the message of Christ's coming to earth carried them through uncertain times. They were astounded by the truth that Jesus, the Son of God, came from the edge of the universe, from above the stars and all galaxies, and arrived on earth in the womb of a virgin named Mary. They were amazed that he grew for nine months like every other baby, and on one ordinary cold winter's night, he was born in the flesh. This truth strengthened their hearts in their suffering, and in our trials and tribulations, it is a truth that can melt our weary hearts as well.

4

THE GREATEST EXCHANGE IN ALL OF HISTORY

Kelly Gissendaner was on death row for almost two decades for the murder of her husband. She planned the murder and convinced her lover to kidnap her husband and kill him in the woods. Afterward they set the evidence on fire. Their motive was to collect a life insurance policy and receive sole ownership of the house the Gissendaners had just purchased. A jury convicted Kelly of murder for her role in the crime, and after refusing a plea deal, she was given a death sentence.

While she sat on death row, Kelly's entire life changed. She was transformed as she came to understand that Jesus died for her. She encountered the Bible and the truth of the gospel. God worked in her heart to bring her to repentance of her sins and to faith in Christ. The inmate became a student and began to study theology; she completed a full Bible program while in prison. Kelly even reached out to a theologian for counsel and help in understanding the Scriptures—Jürgen Moltmann of Germany. I'm not sure if she knew it at the time, but she was corresponding with one of the most famous theologians of the past century! Already in his late eighties, Moltmann responded to Kelly's questions. They exchanged at least thirty letters over the course of several years. Moltmann even visited her in prison on occasion and flew to the United States to attend Kelly's graduation from the prison theology program.

The fruit of Kelly's transformation was on display for all to see. Kelly began to minister to the other women in prison and led various Bible studies. She counseled women through an air vent and prevented some women from committing suicide. Her impact on the inmates was so profound that dozens of people testified to try to get her sentence changed to life in prison. They had seen her transformation with their very own eyes.

Perhaps the biggest change was that in Christ she found peace in the midst of the storm of death she was facing. She was in awe that Jesus took her place on the ultimate death row. On one occasion she said, "I have learned first-hand that no one, not even me, is beyond redemption through God's grace and mercy. I have learned to place my hope in the God I now know, the God whose plans and promises are made known to me in the whole story of the life, death, and resurrection of Jesus."[1] While she faced continued imprisonment and her impending death, she embraced the wave of her suffering because Jesus faced that wave for her. Her hope was not in her continued breaths in this life, but in her union with Christ in this life and in the next. She was a shipwrecked woman who finally found land.[2]

The Exchange

Though you are likely not a convict on death row like Kelly Gissendaner, we are not as different from her as we would like to think. By meditating on this fact, we can more easily embrace the Rock of Ages that our wave of suffering is carrying us toward. All of us have at one time rejected God. The Bible is clear that we are all under an eternal death sentence, and apart from God's intervention we would all sit on death row facing a forever death. The truth of God's holiness and our sin means we can never be in his presence unless something changes. We are not simply in need of an inspiring example—we need a saving substitute. We need someone who will take our punishment.

Thankfully, Jesus became a substitute for us in a colossal way. On Jesus's final day on this earth he was arrested in a garden and taken for trial. It was a brief ordeal because there was no real evidence. There was no attorney with exhibit *A* or a last-minute witness to take the stand who would clinch the verdict. The three mock trials probably lasted a few minutes each. Jesus bounced from Pilate to Herod and then back to Pilate again.

It was in the final trial that Jesus was sentenced to death. It seems as if Pilate didn't necessarily want to send Jesus to his death, but he bowed down to the pressure of the Jews (Matt. 27:22–24). As the Roman governor over Jerusalem, Pilate already had a difficult relationship with the Jewish population. He previously had remedied a budget shortage by pillaging the temple treasury for funds. The Jews were so angry that many rioted. The soldiers Pilate sent to stop the riot ended up beating many Jews to death. That will certainly make you an enemy of the people. At another point, the Jews were so exasperated with Pilate for decorating his palace with idols, they actually appealed to Caesar. The ruler was less than thrilled at the bickering and asked Pilate to remove the idols. Pilate was supposed to keep the Jews under control, but he just couldn't seem to do it.

Now Pilate faced yet another potentially explosive issue: what to do with Jesus? Another riot would have been costly. With two strikes against him, a third one might put Pilate out of work and on the streets for good. The situation with Jesus came to a boiling point during the Passover. It was tradition that the Roman Empire would allow one convicted felon to go free, and the Jews could choose who this would be. Matthew 27:15–18 records this moment:

> Now at the feast the governor was accustomed to release for the crowd any one prisoner whom they wanted. And they had then a notorious prisoner called Barabbas. So when they had gathered, Pilate said to them, "Whom do you want me to release for you: Barabbas, or Jesus who is called Christ?" For he knew that it was out of envy that they had delivered him up.

Pilate might have said to himself, "Here's my opportunity to simply let Jesus go free. We'll put forward the worst prisoner, a murderer, and we'll put forward Jesus. Surely they won't let the other guy go free." But they did. The chief priests and elders persuaded the crowd to release Barabbas. Pilate was so surprised, he asked them again a second time, "'Which of the two do you want me to release for you?' And they said, 'Barabbas'" (Matt. 27:21). And so just to clarify, Pilate asked them one last time, "'Then what shall I do with Jesus who is called Christ?' They all said, 'Let him be crucified!' And he said, "Why? What evil has he done?' But they shouted all the more, 'Let him be crucified!'" (Matt. 27:22–23).

This whole scenario is surprising to say the least. Jesus had been accused of crimes that could not be proved. Then there was Barabbas who was basically a terrorist. The crowd chose a murderer over the one who brings the dead back to life. They chose evil over the one who loves perfectly. Pilate knew Jesus was innocent, but the crowds roared to free Barabbas and to crucify Jesus. And Pilate caved in to save his job.

I have often wondered what Barabbas was thinking at that point. He was sitting on death row in a Roman prison and certainly aware that he could be killed any day. There was not a clear or straightforward process of parole or further appeals for him to count on. Prisoners didn't have any rights. It was over for him.

There was no hope. He was a murderer who deserved death, and deep down he probably knew it. Each passing day was one day closer to certain death. He may have been imagining it—the flogging, mocking, and eventual death. It was coming.

And then the day comes. He can hear the shouts ringing throughout the courtyard: "Crucify him, crucify him!" Perhaps he was thinking to himself, "They are coming for me." The guards open the door to his cell and drag him outside. But then an astonishing thing happens. Everyone is celebrating his new freedom. His chains are released, and he is set free. The murderer is set free.

Put yourself in his sandals for a minute. You are walking to your death in chains and then all of a sudden, when you least expect it, you are a free man. Then you hear the words begin again: "Crucify him, crucify him." And you see another walking by. Those chants are not for you. The guards are dragging another man to his death—Jesus of Nazareth. He's beaten and flogged and is forced to carry his cross to his death. It's the very cross you had imagined yourself carrying only moments earlier. You think to yourself, that's my death he's dying. Barabbas is the one person in history who could say that Jesus literally carried his cross. Jesus took his death, and Barabbas was given the freedom Jesus deserved. Jesus bore the guilt and shame and curse and disgrace and death that Barabbas deserved. Barabbas received the release, the freedom, and the life that Jesus deserved. It was an incredible scene.[3]

You and I Are Barabbas

I wonder if Barabbas ever got over that moment. You would think that the image of Jesus carrying *his* cross would have been etched on his mind and heart for the rest of his life. There are too many ironies for him to miss it. Barabbas's name means "son of the father." Bar means "son" and Abba means "father." In the book of Matthew we learn that his full name was Jesus Barabbas.[4] Jesus, son of the father. Tim Keller points out that we have two Jesuses in our story. Both "son of the Father," and yet they could not be more different. One rules by taking the lives of others, and the other rules by giving his own life. One wants to overthrow the king, and the other is the rightful King of the people. One is guilty and will be set free, and the other is an innocent man who is about to be killed. The real Son of the Father, who is innocent, will go to his death. They freed the wrong son.[5]

Jesus was going to be killed for the kind of crime that the man set free actually committed. The ironies continue. Jesus literally took Barabbas's punishment for him. Jesus even marched to his death as Barabbas would have. Jesus marched willingly and quietly. And yet it wasn't because he had lost. Jesus was not outsmarted by his opponents. This was not a mistake or an accident. It was not plan B in God's eternal plan of salvation. The crucifixion of the innocent Lamb of God was God's plan from eternity past.

In Luke 9 we read that Jesus set his face toward Jerusalem because he was on a mission. His whole life was moving toward Golgotha, toward that hill where he would die. His life was a march toward that cross. He lived to die. Jesus once said, "No one takes [my life] from me, but I lay it down of my own accord" (John 10:18).

The Jews chose the wrong man, but the Lord put forward the right one. That's the gospel. "For our sake he made him to be sin who knew no sin, so that in him we might become the righteousness of God" (2 Cor. 5:21). You and I are sinners. We sit in a spiritual prison, bound helpless, awaiting the day when we will receive the just punishment we deserve. We sit on the death row of all death rows waiting to be dragged out to death not knowing when God's righteous judgment will come down. But the good news is that when you repent of your sin and trust in Jesus to save you, Jesus goes off to the cross in your place. He gets what you deserve; you get what he deserves. It is the greatest exchange in all of history. Jesus gives up his life so you can have life.

Joy in our trials can begin to take root in our hearts when we understand the magnitude of grace God has given us. Unless we stand in Barabbas's sandals and find they fit us, we won't see the gravity of God's love for us. This is our story. You and I are Barabbas. We needed someone to take our place, and Jesus has done that for us. He willingly took the wrath of God upon himself. On the cross, Jesus absorbed all our wickedness. He has poured out his perfect love upon us.

First Peter 3:18 says, "For Christ also suffered once for sins, the righteous for the unrighteous, that he might bring us to God, being put to death in the flesh but made alive in the spirit." Jesus was leading a true revolution. You can always stop a Barabbas—you can stop soldiers and eventually halt a military operation. You can raid the captain's headquarters and take him down. But you can't stop Jesus. He took our place on the cross so that the greatest exchange in all of history would bring you to God.

Our Joy—Now

It is tempting to treat the cross like an admission ticket to the theater. We purchase the ticket and keep it in a safe place until the evening of the event, when we will retrieve it to be admitted to the performance. In a similar way, many of us live as if believing the gospel is our entrance ticket into heaven. We wholeheartedly believe we will enjoy the benefits of Christ's death on the cross when we die. But something is massively missing if we leave the benefits of the cross to eternity. When we do that, we create what Timothy Lane and Paul Tripp call a "Gospel Gap."[6] Rather than remembering and relying on the gospel in all things, we fill the gap with other lesser promises or by doing things that we think will make us happy—even good things.

We tend to underestimate the benefits of the cross for us today. The cross not only guarantees entry into heaven, it's also our forever ticket to eternal joy, starting today. The cross of Christ is what we need to rejoice in today, tomorrow, and every day until we breathe our last breath. Being freed from death like Barabbas, we are now free from the crippling fear of the present. We are helped in our loneliness because we realize we have a friend who will never betray or abandon us.

The great exchange means we can begin each day by reminding ourselves that though we suffer, we are sinners saved by grace. We can say things to ourselves such as:

- Though I am ashamed as I contemplate my sinful past, as far as the east is from the west, that's how far my sin is from me (Ps. 103:12).
- Though I think there is no hope in this season of life, I will remember that there is now no condemnation for me in Christ Jesus (Rom. 8:1).
- Though my trouble is overwhelming today, the cross shows me that because God is for me, who can be against me (Rom. 8:31)?
- Though the waves of my trials threaten to drown me, who will separate me from the love of God in Christ Jesus (Rom. 8:35)?
- Though I can't stop crying today, I know there is coming a day when Christ will be with us and he will wipe away every tear from our eyes. Death will no longer exist and all crying and anxiety will cease (Rev. 21:4).

When we remind ourselves of the greatest exchange in our trials, we fill in that gospel gap with the good news of Jesus.

We do what Martin Lloyd-Jones said and preach the gospel to ourselves. Rather than dwelling on our circumstances, which are always changing, we dwell on the truth of this exchange. We infuse this truth in our heart, mind, and soul. Lloyd-Jones challenges us to think this way:

> I say that we must talk to ourselves instead of allowing "ourselves" to talk to us! . . . Have you realized that most of your unhappiness in life is due to the fact that you are listening to yourself instead of talking to yourself? Take those thoughts that come to you the moment you wake up in the morning. You have not originated them, but they start talking to you, they bring back the problems of yesterday, etc. Somebody is talking. Who is talking to you? Your self is talking to you. . . . The main art in the matter of spiritual living is to know how to handle yourself. You have to take yourself in hand, you have to address yourself, preach to yourself, question yourself. You must say to your soul: "Why are you cast down" . . . and say to yourself: "Hope in God"—instead of muttering in this depressed, unhappy way. And then you must go on to remind yourself of God, Who God is, and what God is and what God has done, and what God has pledged Himself to do.[7]

When struggling through trials, allow everything in your life to point you to the cross. When you are downcast, go on the offensive and preach to yourself. Not all of us are called to preach the gospel to a church on a Sunday morning, but all of us are called to preach truth to our own hearts each day. Remind yourself that God so loved you that he gave his one and only Son over to the cross for you. In your pain, preach to yourself that it should have been you up there on the cross, but that in the greatest exchange in all of history, he went there instead. Other truths can bring you some measure of joy, but why not remind yourself of and reflect on the greatest news in all the world? Why look for lesser truths to bring you hope in your pain than the most joy-inflicting, radical reminder that Jesus went to the cross in your place?

This is what Kelly Gissendaner relentlessly worked to do as she sat on death row. After a number of attempts to halt her execution and a couple of procedural delays, Kelly Gissendaner was finally executed by the state. It is said that even in her final moments she was "preaching" the gospel of Jesus Christ to herself. Witnesses could hear her praying and singing loudly with joy. The microphone was turned off, but her voice passed through the glass window and all could hear her clearly singing the first verse of John Newton's "Amazing Grace."[8]

> Amazing grace! How sweet the sound
> That saved a wretch like me!
> I once was lost, but now am found;
> Was blind, but now I see.

Even at the end Kelly could not get over what God had done for her. I love what Moltmann once said about her: "If the state of Georgia has no mercy—she has received already the mercy of Heaven."[9] Kelly Gissendaner, a murderer, was not beyond the grace of God. God can save murderers.

The apostle Paul, persecutor and murderer of the children of God, is not beyond the grace of God. You and I are not beyond his grace.

Friend, don't forget this in your pain.

5

JESUS IS RAISED

Childbirth is an extremely painful process. I've obviously never given birth to a child, but I have been present during the births of my four children. The pain of giving birth consumes the mother. During the hours of labor, she can't consider anything else besides what is happening with her body.

If I hadn't fully realized this from the birth of our first three children, I certainly learned this during the birth of our fourth. Two weeks before the due date of our little one, Gloria and I had settled down for the night to do some reading. Gloria started to feel sick and told me that she was going to call her doctor to see what kind of medicine she could take. In the middle of her conversation with her doctor, her demeanor changed dramatically, and she doubled over while pleading with the doctor on the phone, "Help me, help me!" The doctor told my wife to hang up the phone and meet her at the hospital immediately.

I'm no medical professional, but I realized at that point that we were probably going to have our baby that night. I quickly slipped on my sandals and started doing the first task I had been charged to do in preparation for the baby's arrival: call a babysitter to come watch our three sleeping kids. I did that, and I was ready to do the next thing I was responsible for: go downstairs and find a taxi.

That's when I noticed that Gloria wasn't getting ready to leave. In fact, she wasn't doing anything. I asked her what I could do to help her. She just yelled at me: "Just pray!" I thought to myself, "Prayer is good, but isn't there something I should do to help right now?"

Then Gloria yelled out, "The baby is coming." Of course the baby is coming, I thought. That's why we needed to go downstairs to catch a taxi.

I didn't realize that she meant the baby was coming *now*!

What happened next is a blur to me, but in a few seconds Gloria gave birth to a baby boy that I helped deliver all by myself in our apartment.

Many friends have remarked how great it was that Gloria had already given birth to three other children and that her knowledge as a doula (someone who helps women give birth) allowed her to help me deliver our child. Actually, my wife could not and did not do a single thing to help me. I stood there absolutely terrified and did not receive any instructions from her. When a woman is in the middle of the agony of childbirth, she can't think about anything else, much less give calm, orderly instructions to the people around her. It's impossible. Her focus is singular, and her distress is too great.

But then, in the midst of the worst pain imaginable, everything suddenly changes. The baby is born, and agony turns into joy. In the same way, for a believer, a life filled with heartache will one day turn from tragedy to triumph.

Greatest Hope in the World

It was hours before the crucifixion, and the disciples were gathered in the upper room. Jesus was preaching his last discourse to them, and he challenged them to be servants. As an example to them, he washed his own disciples' feet. He urged them to abide in the vine and walk with God all the days of their lives. Then Jesus assured them that while pain is imminent, it will be short-lived. Jesus shared hope-filled words:

> Truly, truly, I say to you, you will weep and lament, but the world will rejoice. You will be sorrowful, but your sorrow will turn into joy. When a woman is giving birth, she has sorrow because her hour has come, but when she has delivered the baby, she no longer remembers the anguish, for joy that a human being has been born into the world. So also you have sorrow now, but I will see you again, and your hearts will rejoice, and no one will take your joy from you. (John 16:20–22)

When the baby is born, everything changes. After the delivery of our son, Gloria instantly turned from Momzilla (slight exaggeration, but mostly true) into Supermom. At the moment when I had to try to support the full weight of the baby in my disabled arms, she lifted the infant from my hands and cradled him. She helped him breathe and was completely cognizant of all that needed to be done.

I called the doctor and was instructed to call an ambulance (not a taxi!) and to tie off the umbilical cord with something sterile. I placed the emergency call and brought Gloria a brand-new tennis shoe. She used her free arm to cut off the clean laces and tie the cord (a pretty amazing ninja-like move). Anxiety and fear had turned to hope and happiness. Both my wife and child were delivered through the pain of labor and birth. The dread and uncertainty of the moments prior felt like a distant memory as we held onto our bundle of joy.

Jesus told the disciples that much like a mom's agony of childbirth is forgotten when her baby is born, so too their anguish would disappear when he resurrected from the dead. This joy would be so great and unchangeable that no one could take it away (John 16:22). True joy is a joy that is not subject to ever-changing circumstances.

It is a joy that is grounded in truth. As we suffer, we can work hard to try to numb our painful circumstances or try to deny that they exist. But what we need instead of denial or distraction is a truth that will overwhelm the trouble. In the resurrection we have that truth and it cannot be undone. It means that everything Jesus said and did was trustworthy.

Because Jesus rose from the dead, we know that every promise he made will be fulfilled. We know that everything he said will come true. There will be a final accounting; an actual time is coming when evil will be once and for all defeated. All of God's children will attend the funeral of death, because death is going to die. Mercy will reign forever.

And so you and I can have hope in this world regardless of what trial we are enduring.

The Resurrection Means Your Sins Are Forgiven

Paul writes one of the clearest short descriptions of the gospel in the Bible in his first letter to the Corinthians:

> If there is no resurrection of the dead, then not even Christ has been raised. And if Christ has not been raised, then our preaching is in vain and your faith is in vain. . . . And if Christ has not been raised, your faith is futile and you are still in your sins. (1 Cor. 15:13–14, 17)

Paul says that the resurrection is not just a part of the Christian faith; it's not something that just happened alongside other more important things. The resurrection is of extraordinary importance because if it didn't happen and Christ is dead, then our faith is in vain. Our gatherings on Sunday mornings would be hopeless. If Christ has risen, then nothing else on earth can compete with Christ. If Christ hasn't risen and this is the only life there is, then nothing else matters.[1] We are all going to die, and there is no hope for life after death. But if death could not hold Jesus down and he rose from the dead, then we worship him because this world has nothing better to offer us.

The resurrection is absolutely crucial. This is why Paul says that he was passing on something "of first importance": "That Christ died for our sins in accordance with the Scriptures, that he was buried, that he was raised on the third day" (1 Cor. 15:3–4).

Friend, if you are a follower of Christ, the resurrection means your sins are forgiven. You have been reconciled to God. Christ's resurrection means that the sacrifice was complete. Your greatest reality isn't your illness or your sorrow, but that you will be with God forever. You may feel physical pain now, but you will not feel the ultimate pain of facing the wrath of God forever. You will not face the penalty for your sin, because Jesus took that penalty (death) for you so you could be made right with God. All this was proven to be true because Jesus rose from the dead.

The Resurrection Gives Us Hope of New Bodies

On that Sunday morning two thousand years ago, a group of women carrying burial spices went to the garden tomb. They expected to find the dead body of their friend Jesus. Instead, they found the stone rolled away from the entrance of his tomb. When the women looked into the tomb, they saw that Jesus was gone. Instead of a dead body there were angels who told the ladies that Jesus had risen from the dead. Peter—who raced to see this for himself immediately after hearing the report from the ladies—was instantly transformed. For all who heard and believed this news, everything about their future changed.

If you know that this is not the only world, the only body, the only life—that one day you will have a perfect life—you will be able to persevere through any type of adversity. There is hope on the other side, and there will be calm after the storm. Paul writes:

> So we do not lose heart. Though our outer self is wasting away, our inner self is being renewed day by

> day. For this light momentary affliction is preparing for us an eternal weight of glory beyond all comparison, as we look not to the things that are seen but to the things that are unseen. For the things that are seen are transient, but the things that are unseen are eternal. (2 Cor. 4:16–18)

The resurrection gives us hope. It confirms that this life isn't the end of our story. We will be raised with Christ with new bodies. As I type, I feel the spasms in my trembling arms. But I have hope that just as Jesus rose from the dead, he will raise me also. The resurrection is God's ultimate answer to our suffering. Life forever with Christ is our hope. Paul says that our resurrection bodies will be imperishable, glorious, powerful, and spiritual—and we will be changed in the twinkling of an eye.

> I tell you this, brothers: flesh and blood cannot inherit the kingdom of God, nor does the perishable inherit the imperishable. Behold! I tell you a mystery. We shall not all sleep, but we shall all be changed, in a moment, in the twinkling of an eye, at the last trumpet. For the trumpet will sound, and the dead will be raised imperishable, and we shall be changed. For this perishable body must put on the imperishable, and this mortal body must put on immortality. When the perishable puts on the imperishable, and the mortal puts on immortality, then shall come to pass the saying that is written:
>
> > "Death is swallowed up in victory."
> > "O death, where is your victory?

> O death, where is your sting?"
>
> The sting of death is sin, and the power of sin is the law. But thanks be to God, who gives us the victory through our Lord Jesus Christ. (1 Cor. 15:50–57)

I love the story of how Christian author and speaker Joni Eareckson Tada's perspective on life changed when she understood the resurrection. Now in her sixties, Tada was paralyzed in a diving accident when she was seventeen and has lived out her life in a wheelchair. She recounts a moment of crisis when, at a Christian conference, the speaker urged people to get down on their knees to pray. Hundreds of people got down on their knees, but not Joni. She was stuck in her chair.

At first, she cried at the thought of not being able to kneel. But soon her tears became a response to the beautiful scene of hundreds of women on their knees. She thought about the resurrection. She understood that Christ's resurrection meant that she too would be resurrected and given a new body. She realized that when she gets to the wedding feast of the Lamb, the first thing she'll do is to quietly kneel at the feet of Jesus and worship him, and then, she says, "I'll get to dance."[2] The truth of the resurrection gives us real hope.

If you can't kneel and you can't dance and you can't run, in the resurrection you will do all these perfectly.

If you are lonely, in the resurrection you will have perfect love.

If your heart is empty, in the resurrection you will be thoroughly filled.

If you are depressed, in the resurrection your joy will be complete.

Christian, if you are facing grave illness or even death, the resurrection gives you hope that in the moment you die, you will be with Christ.

Don't Forget the Resurrection

While in a seminary, I had to write a paper explaining the gospel. It seemed easy enough. Of course I knew the gospel, and I took great care in writing my paper. If you're a student now, or can remember when you were one, you know the feeling of thinking you did so well on an assignment that you can't wait to learn what your professor thinks about your work. I couldn't wait to get my paper back with a big shiny *A* at the top of it. I knew I had written quite possibly the best paper in the history of evangelism class, and I was ready to be crowned the "king of evangelism." I went to my mailbox to pick up my assignment, pulled out my paper, and turned it over. At the top of it was a big red *F*. I couldn't believe it. I flipped to the back and read the explanation. In big block letters the teacher wrote: "Jesus is still dead? You forgot the resurrection!"

After looking through my paper a couple of times with the intent of proving my professor wrong, I realized that he was right. It wasn't there. The professor rejected my gospel presentation paper because if there is no resurrection, then there is no good news.

Remember the resurrection. Consider that Jesus is no longer in the grave. God raised him from the dead. Paul writes: "But we do not want you to be uninformed, brothers, about those who are asleep, that you may not grieve as others do who have no hope. For since we believe that Jesus died and rose again, even so, through Jesus, God will bring with him those who have fallen asleep" (1 Thess. 4:13–14).

We grieve, but not as those without hope. Your tears are not hopeless tears. Your hope is not grounded in your circumstances but in Jesus. No one can take away your joy. The joy that comes through Christ because of the resurrection is a forever joy. It is not contingent on your circumstances or your health.

Because of the resurrection, you have a relationship with God. He is alive, and he is with you. Consider John's picture of Jesus at the end of his Gospel. Jesus appears to the disciples for a third time.

He fills their net with fish and tells them: "Come and have breakfast" (John 21:12). And then they eat together. I love that simple, beautiful image of fellowship with Jesus. They could have been doing a thousand other things. There was work to do, fish to catch, people to save, sermons to preach. Yet the first thing the disciples do is sit with Jesus, and Jesus delights in them.

That scene reminds me of our Easter celebrations on the beach here in Dubai. Every Easter, we have the privilege of gathering with hundreds of other believers on the beach to watch the sun rise over the desert and celebrate the Son who has risen. The tallest building in the world is nearby, and the Arabian Gulf is behind us. It's the only time of the year when I get to preach barefoot in the sand! But most of all, there on the beach, I have a vivid reminder that we can never get over the resurrection. We never forget it, because if we don't have the resurrection, we don't have hope. I'm glad

I received an *F* for my paper, because I've never forgotten the resurrection since.

Christian, if you are suffering, this is not the end of your story. One day, Jesus will wipe away every tear from your face. I know he will, because he is alive.

6

LOOK, I AM YOUR FATHER

Our family served alongside our good friends, Glen and Donita for the first decade of our church plant in Dubai. We enjoyed sweet moments where we watched lives changed by the gospel, and had our share of memories and laughs.

Along our journey together, the Lord put on Glen and Donita's hearts to adopt two children from Ethiopia. This began another journey for them and our entire church. The whole family worked hard to raise the needed funds, prayed for the children, filled out endless forms, and waited on paperwork to be processed. Months later they were matched and met their children on a visit to Ethiopia. They were excited and couldn't wait to bring their children home.

Along the way they experienced numerous delays in the adoption process. The Ethiopian courts actually stopped processing adoptions on a number of occasions. And so they waited. And waited.

And then waited even longer.

Did I mention that they waited?

It seemed as if they encountered roadblock after roadblock. Everything that could go wrong seemed to go wrong. It was agonizing for them to wait on the finalization of the adoption of these children they had already met and played with. They had fed them and held them in their arms and wanted nothing more than to bring these two beautiful babies into their family. Glen and Donita set their heart and affections on these children and were desperate to shower them with their love.

More Loved Than We Could Imagine

When you believe in Jesus for salvation, there is justification—you are made righteous before God. You are also regenerated—born again. But there is even more that happens when you are saved. When you become a believer in Christ, you are brought into God's family. This is incredibly exciting. We Christians are adopted by God.

John Murray in his classic work, *Redemption Accomplished and Applied,* writes,

> Adoption is an act of God's grace distinct from and additional to the other acts of grace involved in the application of redemption . . . it is particularly important to remember that it is not the same as justification or regeneration. Too frequently it has been regarded as simply an aspect of justification or as another way of stating the privilege conferred by regeneration. It is much more than either or both of these acts of grace . . . by adoption the redeemed become sons and daughters of the Lord God Almighty:

> they are introduced into and given the privileges of God's family. Neither justification nor regeneration expresses precisely that.[1]

When we believe in Christ, we are made right with God. We are saved. But what Murray is saying is that we are actually saved *into* a family. It is a remarkably comforting truth that we are adopted into the family of God. All of us yearn to be in a safe and fulfilling earthly family. Many of us enjoy this to some degree, and yet others of us have such destructive families that one could hardly call it a family at all. But for all of us who come to Christ, we are a part of the greatest family in the world. John 1:12 says, "But to all who did receive him, who believed in his name, he gave the right to become children of God." When we follow Jesus, we (former enemies of God) are not only saved, but saved into his family. Consider these stunning verses about our adoption:

> The Spirit himself bears witness with our spirit that we are children of God, and if children, then heirs—heirs of God and fellow heirs with Christ. (Rom. 8:16–17)

> For in Christ Jesus you are all sons of God, through faith. (Gal. 3:26)

> He predestined us for adoption to himself as sons through Jesus Christ, according to the purpose of his will. (Eph. 1:5)

> See what kind of love the Father has given to us, that we should be called children of God; and so we are. (1 John 3:1)

These verses are simply breathtaking. Just as children are heirs of their earthly father, we are heirs of God!

Murray writes that when we are adopted, "We are transferred from an alien family into the family of God himself. This is surely the apex of grace and privilege. We would not dare to conceive of such grace far less to claim it apart from God's own revelation and assurance. It staggers imagination because of its amazing condescension and love."[2] It may not *feel* this way when you are in pain, but the truth is that as a follower of Jesus you are far more loved than you could ever imagine. You are a part of God's forever family. When waves of trial come crashing down on you and your burden seems unbearable, God remains your Father who takes care of you in those moments. As a child of God, you are adopted into a loving Father-child relationship with him. It would have been astonishing if he simply forgave us for our sin, but God goes further than that. Believer, God has made you his own child—a son or daughter of the Most High.

This truth can especially help us in times of depression and suicidal thoughts. You may think you're not worth anything and no one cares about you, but your heavenly Father had his heart set on you before the foundations of the earth. He adopted you and loves you. We must always live in light of our sonship. When you were brought into God's family, you were given a new name: son or daughter in Christ Jesus. The whole world around you may shake, but your heavenly Father holds you safe in his arms.

He Cares for His Children

If you have been adopted by God, your worth is even more staggering than the love parents have for their children. He wants you not only to know that truth but also to feel it. He wants you to experience it every day.

Puritan preacher Thomas Goodwin depicted the enjoyment of adoption by describing a man "walking along a road with his little boy, holding hands—father and son, son and father. The little boy knows that this man is his father, and that his father loves him. But suddenly the father stops, picks up the boy, lifts him up into his arms, embraces him and kisses him. Then he puts him down again, and they continue walking. . . . The father's action has not changed the relationship . . . but oh, the difference in the enjoyment!"[3]

The father's action has not changed the status of the relationship, but it has changed the experience and enjoyment of it.[4] Like any good parent, God wants his children to know for certain they are beloved, which is one of the reasons God sent his Spirit into our hearts. Adoption was planned by the Father, accomplished by the Son, and applied by the Spirit.

Paul writes in his letter to the Galatians, "And because you are sons, God has sent the Spirit of his Son into our hearts, crying, 'Abba! Father!'" (Gal. 4:6). This is a marvelous truth and one of the most beautiful adoption-related verses in Scripture. It's like a bottomless treasure chest that you could spend all your life digging into. The Aramaic word *Abba* means "Father" but in a more intimate sense. Today we would say *Daddy* or *Papa*.[5] Jesus always addresses the Father this way in his prayers. Now, Paul says, the Spirit is moving in our hearts to cry out the same thing. This is something like when I hug my son Judson, and I lean over and whisper in his ear, "You're my special buddy." He usually responds to those words by giving me a big hug and saying, "You are the best daddy. I love you." This is a small picture of the loving assurance the Father gives his children through the Spirit.[6] Philip Ryken writes, "The Son brings us to the Father and sets us in his lap. The Holy Spirit is the divine whisperer who tells us that we will always be God's special children. When we hear the Spirit's whisper our hearts cry out to God, I love you Father."[7]

Children don't doubt their parents will help them. A child assumes he or she is important and loved. Children simply expect a parent to act on their behalf. No child backs up her request for something with the disclaimer: "Well, now, if you don't mind, Mommy, would it be too much trouble for you to please pour me some apple juice? Or is there a better time to ask to get your help?" I have recently taken a poll of the universe, and there has never been a child who has asked that! Children just know that parents love them and that parents can be trusted, and so they simply ask. And have you ever seen a good dad say, "Only if you do this or that, then I'll feed you breakfast before school. Otherwise, no food for you!"?

Paul addresses the Galatian church by saying, "Because you are sons" (4:6). It's done. As a Christian, you have that status, and you can now approach your Father.

Talking to Our Father

Part of God's love for us and being adopted into his family means that we can talk to our loving Father anytime. During his Sermon on the Mount, Jesus spoke against the Pharisees who would pray in public in order to receive the praise of man (Matt. 6:5–6). They wanted to look holy and righteous and at times would stand on the street corners trying to appear religious. They cared more about people's praise than about God's approval and a relationship with him. In light of this, Jesus instructs his disciples against repetitious and rote prayer. Prayer is not an action simply to check off your to-do list or something we do to impress others—including God. D. A. Carson says, "Jesus' point is that his disciples should avoid meaningless, repetitive prayers offered under the misconception that mere length will make prayers efficacious."[8] Our Father is aware of our needs, and while we should surely share some of those details, we should more importantly share our hearts.

It's an honor to share our hearts with our Father. Prayer is not merely something we must do as Christians; it's something we have the privilege of doing because of our adoption by the Father. Jesus models prayer for us later in this same chapter:

> Our Father in heaven,
> hallowed be your name.
> Your kingdom come,
> your will be done,
> on earth as it is in heaven.
> Give us this day our daily bread,
> and forgive us our debts,
> as we also have forgiven our debtors.
> And lead us not into temptation,
> but deliver us from evil. (Matt. 6:9–13)

The personal nature of the beginning of the model prayer reminds us that we can go to God specifically because he is our Father. Though he is a transcendent God, using this name in prayer reminds us that God is also near. This prayer reminds us that God's name should be revered, that he will bring in his kingdom, and that he is in control over all things, including the forgiveness of our sins.

The last three petitions are also very personal. They remind us of the times when we've approached our earthly father in need. There is prayer for daily bread—food to sustain our life. Back in Christ's days on earth, it was not uncommon to get paid daily, and so the worker would literally have to trust God each day for the provision of food. A lengthy sickness could derail a family. Jesus shows us that this prayer is for our needs, not our greeds.[9] We don't come to God to get rich and famous; we come to God for our daily provision, much like children do with their parents.

Horatius Bonar writes, "In our adoption we are elevated to creation's highest level. We are brought into the inner circle of the Father's love—nearer His throne, nearer His heart than angels."[10] We can talk with God as his children, because we *are* his children. Friend in pain, your Father cares for you. Speak to him through the tears of depression and discouragement. When the nights are long and impossible, cry out to him. When you lie in the hospital awaiting another surgery and test result, ask him to hold you in his arms. When you suffer a miscarriage and feel hopeless, remember that your loving Father is carrying you through the heartache and hears your cries. Your Father is with you, and you are a part of his forever family.

After almost three years, our friends Glen and Donita received word that the Ethiopian courts had stamped their adoption applications with approval. Within hours, our friends were on a flight to Addis Ababa to bring their son and daughter home. It was quite the celebration when they returned. Their other children were excited about the new additions. The church jumped in to help with cooking, cleaning, and schooling. These sweet babies were now part of a new family, receiving affection and love from their parents. The financial strain, the hours of hard work in preparation, the several trips to Africa, the waiting, and the countless prayers had been trying, but they were worth it. This is a small picture, a shadow of what God has done for us. As a believer in Christ you are now adopted into God's family through the death and resurrection of Jesus Christ. It was costly to bring you and me into his family, but— praise God!—the adoption is complete. Through every trial you face and every wave that comes your way, you have a Father who is right there with you in your struggle. He's not detached and distant, but he knows your pain and never stops setting his love upon you.

We need to remember our adoption. Our first thought on an anxious or depressing morning should be, "My Father is with me this day." When you come to the end of the day and your body aches with searing pain, remember that God is aware of your sorrow. When you are in trouble, know that your heavenly Father always takes care of his children. You can cast all your cares on him, because he actually, truly cares. We cannot overstate the loving concern our Father has for us, his children. We could meditate on this for an eternity and never finish considering it. Thankfully, we'll have that opportunity.

7

HE REALLY KNOWS EVERY HAIR ON YOUR HEAD

I read a newspaper article about a woman who tumbled into the bay in Melbourne, Australia. She walked right off St. Kilda's Pier and straight into the water. Police were alerted to the incident and rescued her in a speedboat after about twenty minutes. She didn't know how to swim but, remarkably, was able to float on her back until she was rescued. When the police approached her, they noticed she still had her mobile phone in her hand as she struggled to stay above water. She apologized for all the trouble and confessed that she was checking her Facebook profile on her phone when she walked off the pier and plunged into the water.

The police officer used this opportunity to say that people should pay more attention when using social media around water. The officer had a great point, even if he sounds like Captain Obvious: don't look at your Facebook page when you're walking at the edge of a pier. That sounds like good advice to me![1]

We may be attached or even addicted to the Internet and to social media for various reasons. Many of us can't put our phones down because we are absorbed with being known. We care too much about what people think of us. We are consumed with whether people notice us, so our lives are dominated by this quest. We check our status updates for comments, we watch the "likes" add up on our photos, and we wait for interactions. This is very hard work. You have to select the right picture to share, craft the perfect tweet, and edit your status to your liking.

Our quest for others' approval is symptomatic of a deeper problem. We long to escape the reality of life in a fallen world. We see this when we go through trials, whether physical or emotional pain. We're tempted to escape reality by searching for earthly consolation. We yearn for a friend to notice us. We want nothing more than for our spouses to tell us they are sorry we are sick. We think the attention of others is going to make us happy, or at least dull the pain. But ultimately we are disappointed. The right person doesn't notice our status update. Our spouses don't pick up on our feelings of insecurity. Our friends are busy with their own lives, and they forget about ours. And even when we do get the attention from others that we think we need so desperately, at the end of the day we still feel restless and empty. No relationship is going to give us what our hearts desire 100 percent of the time.

We want to be known. That's OK. In fact, we were made with that desire. The problem is that we often search for significance in the wrong places. This becomes more and more obvious in the midst of our trials.

A God-Shaped Hole

All of us want to be known in some way or another. We may yearn for others to acknowledge our careers, our gifts, or even our struggles. The problem is that when we look to others to fill our malnourished hearts, we find ourselves hungry for still more. Philosopher Blaise Pascal once wrote:

> What else does this craving, and this helplessness, proclaim but that there was once in man a true happiness, of which all that now remains is the empty print and trace? This he tries in vain to fill with everything around him, seeking in things that are not there the help he cannot find in those that are, though none can help, since this infinite abyss can be filled only with an infinite and immutable object; in other words by God himself.[2]

Inspired by Pascal's writing, many have said that you and I were made with a God-shaped hole in our hearts that only God can fill, and that is essentially what Pascal was saying. We look to the world to fill our hearts with security and significance, but even the greatest earthly delights can't fill that hole in our hearts. When we put our hope in this world to give us our source of identity, the world will always fail us. We always end up empty. Being known by God is the only thing that can bring us ultimate satisfaction.

In my disability, I am tempted to work tirelessly to fill that hole with what I think will heal me of my handicap, or at least relieve it. I want all those around me to fully understand the darkness I am going through. I want people to really "know" me. Deep down I want them to understand my affliction and to comfort me with their recognition that what I am going through is terrible. I want people to make much of me and even honor me as one who is dealing with affliction and has it so much worse than everyone else. I want verbal "likes" and "retweets" that show me I'm not forgotten. I want people to remember that I have very little use of my arms and am in constant pain. I want people to know that my life isn't easy and that nights are long and arduous as I wait for the sun to rise. This pursuit of being known and understood is what brings me the greatest conflict in my marriage. If my wife doesn't seem to understand my pain or acknowledge it in the ways I think she should, my anger comes out in full display. But at the end of the day (or night), my efforts to be known are like putting a Band-Aid on a gunshot wound. They are ridiculous, and they do nothing to ultimately heal me of my pain. When I look to other people to bring me consolation or attention, I enter a never-ending, crazy cycle. My heart is never filled.

It's a Miracle That God Chose Us

The morning I introduced a new sermon series on 1 Peter, I had no idea what the response of our church would be. The first two verses teach the controversial doctrine of election—that truth that God chooses those whom he will save. I wondered whether some people would be angry that our church believed this theology. However, my fears were alleviated after the service when a group of a dozen people who were visiting for the first time came up to me and said, "Pastor, we were jumping up and down in our seats during the sermon. When we heard the truth that God would choose and save undeserving sinners for salvation in his Son, we were very excited—this is *very* good news!"

These newcomers experienced firsthand how the doctrine of the sovereignty of God in salvation is food for our souls and fuel for our worship. Our identity is not from anything in this world; we are chosen by God. Being known by God is first to be chosen by God. This is a primary truth that must enter our hearts if we are to find joy in our sorrows.

This idea of God's choosing his people for salvation consumed the biblical writers. Here's what Paul wrote the Thessalonians: "For we know, brothers loved by God, that he has chosen you, because our gospel came to you not only in word, but also in power and in the Holy Spirit and with full conviction" (1 Thess. 1:4–5). Paul doesn't say they were chosen because they were receptive. He says that they received the gospel because *God chose them*.

In Acts 13, many Gentiles come to believe in Christ: "And when the Gentiles heard this, they began rejoicing and glorifying the word of the Lord, and as many as were appointed to eternal life believed" (v. 48).

As many as were appointed believed. It doesn't say that those who believed were thereby appointed, but that those appointed *then* believed.

Jesus says in the Upper Room Discourse: "You did not choose me, but I chose you" (John 15:16). Our choosing of God is based on God's choosing of us, not the other way around.

Ephesians 1 says, "He chose us in him before the foundation of the world" (v. 4). When did God choose us? Before we were born, and before the foundations of the world were even set in place. This is all a miracle because God knew the depth of our sin. God is all-powerful and knows what the future holds. He tells Isaiah the prophet:

> Remember this and stand firm,
> recall it to mind, you transgressors,
> remember the former things of old;
> for I am God, and there is no other;
> I am God, and there is none like me,
> declaring the end from the beginning
> and from ancient times things not yet done,
> saying, "My counsel shall stand,
> and I will accomplish all my
> purpose." (Isa. 46:8–10)

God knew what the future held when he created us. And Romans says, "For if while we were enemies we were reconciled to God by the death of his Son, much more, now that we are reconciled, shall we be saved by his life" (Rom. 5:10). This is the true miracle.

This truth of God's choosing us brings great comfort for the hurting. One of the reasons Peter mentions this truth at the very beginning of his letter was to comfort the persecuted Christians in their distress. And the men and women Paul was writing to in Rome were losing everything because of their faith. Paul was also reminding them of this truth: "Who shall bring any charge against God's elect?" The answer is: "It is God who justifies" (Rom. 8:33). The answer is: It is God who justifies. Nobody can bring a charge. Satan can't make a single charge against God's chosen ones. God is the one who justifies them. There is now nothing to fear. Let this sink into your weary heart.

The Cinderella of Theology

Believer, God took note of you. God chose you. You did nothing to earn his favor, but he has set his affections on you. God has reached down and grabbed his enemies and made them his friends. John Piper writes, "Deeper than knowing God is being known by God. What defines us as Christians is not most profoundly that we have come to know him but that he took note of us and made us his own."[3] Can you handle this truth? Believer in Christ Jesus, God has known and loved you before the foundation of the world. This is a doctrine to be enjoyed, and to comfort us in our heartache.

God's choosing us for salvation is a doctrine that shoots a dart of grace into our hearts when we apply it to our lives. J. I. Packer writes in *Knowing God*:

> What matters supremely, therefore, is not, in the last analysis, the fact that I know God, but the larger fact which underlies it— the fact that *he knows me.* I am graven on the palms of his hands. I am never out of his mind. All my knowledge of him depends on his sustained initiative in knowing me. I know him because he first knew me, and continues to know me. He knows me as a friend, one who loves me; and there is no moment when his eye is off me, or his attention distracted from me, and no moment, therefore, when his care falters.[4]

Is there a greater love story than this? Brian Rosner calls being known by God the "Cinderella of Theology."[5] We bring nothing to the table with God. We have no pedigree that would attract him to us. We have no earthly reason he should look at us, but he does.

Being known by God gives us comfort in the dark nights of the soul. One Puritan called being known by God "the full and final comfort of a believer."[6] Friend, listen to these truths about God knowing you:

> O Lord, you have searched me and *known me*!
> You *know* when I sit down and when I rise up;
> you *discern* my thoughts from afar.
> You *search* out my path and my lying down
> and are *acquainted* with all my ways.
> Even before a word is on my tongue,
> behold, O Lord, you *know* it altogether.
> You *hem* me in, behind and before,
> and lay your hand upon me. (Ps. 139:1–5)

> But you, O Lord, *know me*; you see me, and test my heart toward you. (Jer. 12:3)

> My sheep hear my voice, and I *know* them, and they follow me. (John 10:27)

> For now we see in a mirror dimly, but then face to face. Now I know in part; then I shall know fully, *even as I have been fully known*. (1 Cor. 13:12)

God knows you and what you are going through in your darkest trial. This is a truth I must come back to every day. God knows every time I bump my tender elbows on the side of a door and cry out in agony. He sees every accident. He knows when my leg pain is so bad that I lie awake in bed for hours. He is keenly aware of my feelings of depression and the hopelessness that often rage within my heart. He knows you and your trials. He knows each of your chemotherapy appointments. He was there weeping with you when you lost a loved one. He knows your every injury and irritation. He sees your despair. He knows how you feel.

Rosner points out that during the three lowest points in the history of Israel (slavery in Egypt, the wilderness wandering, and the exile), God reassured his people that he *knew* them. During Israel's greatest trials, God's way of encouraging them was to let them know he hadn't forgotten them. He knew what they were going through. Their trials did not escape his divine gaze.[7]

He Really Does Know Every Hair on Our Heads

In the incarnation Jesus relates to our earthly trials. He faced physical, emotional, and spiritual agony during his life and death on the earth. The one who went through the pain is also the one who knows about our pain. Jesus, when preaching to thousands, told the crowd not to fear:

> I tell you, my friends, do not fear those who kill the body, and after that have nothing more that they can do. But I will warn you whom to fear: fear him who, after he has killed, has authority to cast into hell. Yes, I tell you, fear him! Are not five sparrows sold for two pennies? And not one of them is forgotten before God. Why, even the hairs of your head are all numbered. Fear not; you are of more value than many sparrows. (Luke 12:4–7)

Jesus really knows every hair on your head. I have what looks like thousands of strands of hair on my head (though I am slowly losing some). And Jesus knows them all. Every single one. He knows about every ache, every wound, every thought and emotion. Every bad day is a day Jesus is aware of. No trial surprises him or escapes his eye. Jesus encourages those who are facing persecution to not fear those who can kill the body but do nothing else. Instead we can trust the God who knows us and is keenly aware of all our circumstances.

Jesus is not unaware of the waves that are crashing down on you today. Don't look to find your comfort in anyone else. That aimless pursuit would be like Cinderella at the ball being pursued by the prince, but leaving the party to try and make herself known to someone else. It would be ridiculous. But this is what we do when we spend our time searching for significance in the things of this world. We have the King of kings who has set his affection on us. He knows us and cares for us, and yet we go off looking for solace in other places.

Hurting friend, don't look for your ultimate comfort in the things in this world. Some of these things are good things, and they are often a help to us, but one day even the good things will fail you. Don't look for comfort in your social media activity or your hobbies. Don't search for it among friends from work or in your boss's applause.

You are known by the King. He knows your name and everything about you. He sees all of your pain. In the words of the apostle Paul, "If anyone loves God, he is known by God" (1 Cor. 8:3). The church, the unloveable chosen by God, is the true Cinderella story.

8

OUR PAIN HAS A GLORIOUS PURPOSE

When our church first got started, I used to work out of a room at our home. As I prepared my sermons, I would often look out my window and be motivated by the technological beauty of massive jumbo jets landing at the nearby airport and the simple elegance of the bougainvillea flowers in our garden.

One day I looked out the window and saw the gardener chopping up my beloved bougainvillea bushes. Branches flew everywhere until all the leaves and most of the branches were in a pile surrounding him. The first thought that came to my mind was that we had hired the worst gardener in all of history. I found Gloria and said, “Have you seen what the gardener is doing? He is destroying everything!” It upset me that all the beautiful branches and piles of flowers lay wilting on the ground. It looked as though the gardener had murdered our beautiful bushes.

Obviously, I never took Gardening 101. To the ignorant eye this butcher of the bushes was killing my flowers, but to the knowing eye he was a wise vinedresser. He knew that the life of the bush actually increases with pruning. Weeks later, my sermon preparation was enriched by the view of those once barren branches holding an abundance of beautiful flowers.

Jesus used this analogy when he talked about growth in the Christian life (John 15). He said that spiritual growth often involves a form of suffering. Our goal as followers of Christ should be that we love Jesus more as a result of our pain. As believers, we need to learn to kiss the wave of our trials and embrace God in our suffering because God is working in our hearts to make us more like Christ.

Spiritual Pruning

Before Jesus went to the cross, he gave a final sermon of instruction to his disciples. The sermon is called the Upper Room Discourse, and we find it in John 15. Right in the middle, Jesus uses a gardening metaphor to describe the importance of growing spiritually and drawing strength from him—the true Vine.

> I am the true vine, and my Father is the vinedresser. Every branch in me that does not bear fruit he takes away, and every branch that does bear fruit he prunes, that it may bear more fruit. Already you are clean because of the word that I have spoken to you. Abide in me, and I in you. As the branch cannot bear fruit by itself, unless it abides in the vine, neither can you, unless you abide in me. I am the vine; you are the

> branches. Whoever abides in me and I in him, he it is that bears much fruit, for apart from me you can do nothing. (John 15:1–5)

Jesus was telling the disciples and all Christians that he is setting them apart for a lifestyle of bearing fruit. The branches alone don't produce fruit; fruit is the overflow of life that flows from the vine. The branch has no source of life in itself. It depends completely upon the vine for sustenance.

Jesus also tells us that fruit is a result of suffering. Suffering is described as pruning.

Pruning can be considered an art, because as plants and circumstances vary, gardeners exercise their creativity. But there are some established rules in vinedressing, and it's important to follow the rules for the production of wine. For instance, you don't leave more than two buds for future growth. Grapes never grow on new growth but only on old growth after pruning. The final pruning is not left to amateurs, but is often done by the one who owns the vineyard.[1]

Different vines produce unique varieties of grapes. Like the branches in Jesus's story, we are all different, but God is glorified in all of us in different ways. He will prune us differently, and this is a process we entrust to him. It's been said that "there is a certain kind of maturity that can be attained only through the discipline of suffering."[2] Real maturity happens when we realize that real fruit will never come through our own efforts, but only so much as we are connected to the Vine. In this way, God redeems our suffering in his grace in order to cut off any impurities and cause us to grow.

An Opportunity to Put Away Our Idols

One result of our trials is that suffering often unveils the idols in our lives. Our pain brings an opportunity to see those idols and destroy ones we may never have known were there. One of our old friends likes to tell of a memory that is seared in her mind from when she was twelve years old. She was standing at the back door of her home when her dad took out an ax. He had placed on the ground a beautifully designed, three-foot-tall carved wooden statue of Buddha. He picked up the ax and swung it down, destroying the statue. Then another swing and another, and the statue was reduced to smithereens. The original statue was unrecognizable in the chips of wood.

Up to that day, her family had always showed reverence for the idol. They believed that the idol would prosper them and bring them good fortune as it watched over them. They were to worship it. But after her father placed his faith in Jesus, he realized he had to destroy the idols he had devotedly worshiped his whole life. As the daughter watched her father crush this idol, it became clear that the reality of the gospel demanded the killing of her own idols too.

It's amazing how suffering is a prime time for the revelation of the idols in our hearts. You can't really start turning away from your idolatry if you don't know what your idols are, and yet we are all tempted to love and trust in things other than God. We are all prone to wander from the worship of the one true God. You may not have a totem pole on your property, visit a statue to pray to it, or keep an artifact that you feel brings you good things. But every one of us is tempted to set up idols in our hearts.

One idol many of us struggle with is security and significance in relationships. But we will be crushed if we look for our self-worth in our relationships. If you are crushed every time your spouse fails to give you the love you think you deserve, your spouse may have become a functional idol. You are looking to your spouse to give you what only Christ can give you. During my deepest moments of misery I often looked to Gloria to give me my security and significance. When she didn't serve me or help me in the way I thought I deserved, I was frustrated, angry, and even bitter. The problem is, no person will be able to perfectly fulfill all our needs and wants and desires. They are not meant to. We are all sinners who will let people down. A marriage and all relationships must not be rooted in personal fulfillment but grounded in worship of our King. If Jesus is not the center of your life, in the midst of pain you will self-destruct from your idolatry.

Some good questions to ask yourself in order to identify your potential idols are these: What thing, if you lost it, would make all meaning and significance and hope disappear from your life? What thing, if it were absent, would destroy your life? What's your worst nightmare? Consider it in less dramatic terms: What has the power to ruin your day? The Bible says it could be an idol.[3]

Several idols can appear when we are suffering. Constantly fighting to make it through a day can get in the way of your desire to relax, and your idol of comfort is revealed. The fear of being alone may bring up an idol of security. Dealing with a disability could be a daily reminder that your picture-perfect family life will never happen. The dreams you had for your home might shatter. Maybe your trial brings about insecurity as you constantly wonder what others think about you. You've been relying on your reputation for your significance, but now people are questioning your motives. Maybe you don't know how your next week is going to look, and your idol of control is now obvious. Comfort, security, significance, and control are not bad things. All of these could be good things, but when you are consumed with them, they can become dangerous things. Such idols will never stop demanding your worship and—in the end—they will leave you empty, joyless, and spiritually destitute.

Our Biggest Problem Is Not Outside of Us

In our struggles we are tempted to think that our greatest difficulty exists outside of us and not inside of us. We often blame our environment or our childhood for our behavior. We say things like, "The pressure at work made me do it," or "My spouse irritated me, and so I erupted in anger." "My health or depression is so bad, I have no choice." "This trial I'm going through is just too much for me to handle." "I really can't help myself given my circumstances and all these awful sinners around me are always exasperating me."

I love the illustration the late biblical counselor David Powlison often used to show the relationship between what's in our hearts and what happens around us. He takes out a water bottle filled with water, removes the cap, and starts smashing the bottle, bending it, and spilling water out of it. Water pours on the floor and on his arm, and soon water is all over the place. Powlison then asks, "Why is there water on the floor?" The typical answer is that there is water on the floor because someone shook the bottle. But the ultimate answer, Powlison asserts, is that there is water on the floor because there was water in the bottle. The situation doesn't create the water. In the same way, your circumstances don't create what's in your heart; your situation is just the stage on which the heart's condition is revealed.[4] Perhaps you can relate to some of the following:

- On the way to visit your ailing parent, someone cuts you off in traffic, and you erupt in anger.
- You've been enduring the stress of countless medical treatments, and every word you speak to your children is laced with irritability.
- Your disability or disease has worn you down to the point where you feel you cannot go on any longer.
- In your depression, your family responds callously, and you sink even further into the darkness.

We think we exploded in anger because of our circumstances: "She made me do it—it's not my fault!" But Jesus says, "For out of the abundance of the heart the mouth speaks" (Matt. 12:34). The blaming finger should never be pointed at our circumstances or another person but only at ourselves. Augustine used to pray, "Lord, deliver me from that evil man . . . myself."[5]

Until I began to suffer with the nerve disease in my arms, I didn't know that I was an impatient person. I had no idea I had an anger problem. It wasn't until I was pressed a bit that I found out this aspect of the darkness of my flesh and my sin. For the longest time, I blamed my anger on my pain, and I blamed my impatience on my wife. My idol of comfort (in yearning for health) was elevated over and above everything in my life, and it was destroying me.

Ironic, isn't it? Idols are harsh masters.

My sin was exposed. My circumstances did not cause it, but merely brought out into the open what was already inside my heart. What I had (and still have) was an opportunity to repent. Denying our sin, shifting the blame for our sin, or minimizing our sin will only make things worse and cause our pain to deepen and fester.

Your Suffering Is a Gift

It has been said that "people do not drift toward holiness."[6] Growing in holiness doesn't happen automatically. People don't naturally gravitate toward the things of God. We don't wake up one day and look in the mirror and say, "Well, it looks like I'm finally holy." Growing in holiness takes time and energy. Your trial is an ample time to embrace God and the reality that God is using your pain to make you more like Christ.

Of course, the way to fight through our trials and grow in holiness is what we've talked about all through this book. Growing in holiness doesn't start by trying harder, but by believing better. We need to hope in the future grace we have in Christ, we need to comprehend the dimensions of the love of Christ, and we need to rest in his finished work on the cross. That is what fuels our growth. It has to start there.

With that in mind, ask God to change your heart in your pain. Kevin DeYoung writes, "It's one thing to graduate from college ready to change the world. It's another thing to be resolute in praying that God change you."[7] We are often so consumed with asking God to heal our bodies that we forget to ask him to heal our hearts. We should talk with God about our spiritual life and ask for his help. We need to pursue reading God's Word on a regular basis to remind us of God's work. Read good books that will encourage you in the gospel. Meet up with friends who edify you and point you to the finished work of Christ. Memorize Scripture so you can be thinking about truth when you wake up and when you go to sleep. Consider fasting from food or something else and ask God to bring you to a greater dependence upon him. You won't automatically drift toward holiness in your pain, but there are things you can do to point yourself in the right direction and move toward the better destination.

I often tell those in our church's membership class my prayer for each of them. I don't pray that they would ultimately get promotions, make more money, and be successful in the marketplace (though those aren't necessarily bad things). I pray that they would love Jesus more when they leave Dubai (most of us will not be able to retire here and will have to go home at some point) than they do at that moment. I pray the same for all of us in our trials. In our sickness and suffering, may we all love Jesus more at the end of our agony than we do right now, either when we are healed on this earth or in heaven. That's the measure of success in our trials.

I pray that we would not run away from God or get angry in our trials but that we would see them as a gift. I don't know if you've ever thought about your suffering as a gift. But it is. James 1:2–4 says, "Count it all joy, my brothers, when you meet trials of various kinds, for you know that the testing of your faith produces steadfastness. And let steadfastness have its full effect, that you may be perfect and complete, lacking in nothing."

This is why we embrace God in our suffering. Our trials are an endless buffet table filled with opportunities for us to grow and look more like Christ. As you struggle through your pain, be comforted that God is not wasting this trial but is doing a good work in you during this hard time. We can have joy in our trials because God is working in our hearts. The pruning happening right now in your life is difficult, but it is surely forming you more into the image of Christ. It may feel like you're being chopped up in the storm of your life, but the divine gardener is pruning you so that you bear more fruit in your life than you could ever ask for or imagine.

9

WEAKNESS IS ALWAYS THE WAY

We value human strength and earthly perfection. We admire people for "being strong" when they're mourning a loss. We are proud of friends for "standing tall" in the face of adversity. We put images of our most talented athletes on the covers of magazines. Weakness is looked down upon as unnatural and subpar. It's not something to be exalted, but to be rejected. Only the strong survive.

However, in God's way of doing things this couldn't be further from the truth. This is why I love the ancient Japanese form of art called *Kintsugi*. It involves joining together broken pottery pieces with gold or another precious metal. *Kintsugi* literally means "golden patchwork," which is what this art is all about. The artist takes the broken pieces of pottery—such as cups, bowls, or plates— and puts them together again to form the original items. Rather than hiding the flaws of the pottery, the artist highlights the cracks by sealing them with gold. Brokenness is not hidden but showcased for all to see. The reason why *Kintsugi* is found in museums throughout Japan is because the "broken" art is given more value and revered as more beautiful than a cup or bowl that is unbroken.[1]

God's ways are not our ways. His ways are more like the art of *Kintsugi* than how we normally think about strength and weakness. In his perfect plan, God has chosen to use broken people to do extraordinary things. He has planned to use pain and suffering for our good and his glory in ways beyond our wildest imaginations. In God's plan, weakness is *the* way.[2]

Jars of Clay

Kintsugi reminds me of 2 Corinthians 4, where Paul writes:

> But we have this treasure in jars of clay, to show that the surpassing power belongs to God and not to us. We are afflicted in every way, but not crushed; perplexed, but not driven to despair; persecuted, but not forsaken; struck down, but not destroyed; always carrying in the body the death of Jesus, so that the life of Jesus may also be manifested in our bodies. (2 Cor. 4:7–10)

What an astounding truth! Paul had just spent the previous verses talking about the glorious good news of the gospel. He tells us this is our greatest treasure—"the knowledge of the glory of God in the face of Jesus Christ" (2 Cor. 4:6). Christ died to save sinners. Yes, we have this amazing treasure, but we carry it in jars of clay—our frail and broken bodies. Paul contrasts this gospel treasure with the weakness of those who carry it. The two are very different. The gospel is beautiful, unbreakable, of infinite worth, and powerful. Jars of clay are easily breakable and inexpensive. Our bodies are the same way—easily hurt and subject to disease and decay. Powerless.

One interesting thing about these jars of clay—our bodies—is that they are no accident. Our frail bodies are not a mistake. Our frailty is not a surprise to God nor are we weak as a result of him being powerless to give us stronger bodies. The fall brought disease and death, but through our weakness, God shows off his all-surpassing power—to us and to the world. No one can mistake the jar of clay for producing or having anything to do with the treasure being exalted inside it. It is the pleasure of the jar to hold within it the great treasure, but the glory is not the jar. God wants to make it abundantly clear that the power is not from inside us but from outside of us. If we were steel vessels without blemish or weakness, we might be tempted to think we have no need for God. However, God uses weakness to show our need for dependence upon him.

This Is the Story of the Bible

Throughout the pages of the Bible we see weakness on display. J. I. Packer defines weakness in his grand little book *Weakness Is the Way*: "Weakness is a state of inadequacy, or insufficiency, in relation to some standard or ideal to which we desire to conform."[3] The heroes of the Bible are not strong but inadequate and insufficient. They certainly do not meet the standard set by Marvel comics. They are simply jars of clay that God uses to show the world that he gets all the glory.

- God used lowly and discarded Joseph, the boy once sold into slavery, to save the Israelites from famine.

- He used Moses, the stutterer, to confront Pharaoh and lead God's people out of Egypt.
- Joshua and the Israelites faced the walls of Jericho in what they thought would be their fiercest battle against the Canaanites. Instead, God did the unthinkable and commanded them to walk around the walls for six days and on the seventh day blow their trumpets and shout. And what happened? The walls fell down and Jericho was theirs.
- David, the youngest son of Jesse whom everyone had forgotten about (including his own family) takes down Goliath, the pride of the Philistines, with a slingshot. God chose the least, the weakest, to defeat the best. And that little boy became the greatest earthly king in Israel's history.
- Even Jesus, the very Son of God, came to the earth as a frail human being.

This is the story of the Bible. It is all about a powerful God working in the lives of his weak, dependent, loved people. It is *his* work. All of it.

This Is the Story of Our Lives, Too

"Weakness is how God gets all the glory" is one of the storylines of the Bible, but it's also the story of our lives. Many of our great heroes of the faith struggled with physical and emotional health, but the Lord used them to do great things. Spurgeon struggled with depression and discomfort. John Calvin battled gout much of his life. Countless missionaries faced great trials on the field. These stories are not unique.

God works in this way to make it abundantly obvious that he is the one doing all the work. This is what he did for us as we moved overseas. We came in weakness but had no idea what we would face. Four months earlier I had double arm surgery, and we were hoping for healing. We thought that finally, at last, we would be able to go "all in" with our church planting efforts. Instead, I could hardly do anything, and I was depressed and discouraged. We were coming to the Middle East to plant a church, but God showed us and everyone else that *he* was going to build the church, and it would be built upon Christ. I'm not sure we would have understood this otherwise. I had gone through five years of seminary, several internships, a year of church planting training, cross-cultural training, second language acquisition training, and a host of other equipping opportunities. We spent years in preparation, and we were ready to see revival. I came to change the world, but instead God was changing me. God stripped me of my pride and accomplishments and made it abundantly clear that the church would not grow because of my strength but because of his.

Gloria and I were broken during those nightmare days as we moved overseas, but God's extraordinary power was working in and through us. Those moments drove us to our knees to depend on his grace for everything. We were not only depending on God for the church but simply to get through another night when the pain and depression hung over me like a dark cloud.

False preachers all over the world tell their followers that health and wealth are the blessings God gives to his people if they are faithful. But God never promises a pain-free existence. In a fallen world our reality will often be a pain-full one.

You may have health and wealth at various times (those are not bad things!), but they do not last forever. We are jars of clay. Jars get dented and broken. They get scratched and scraped.

What is most encouraging as we read 2 Corinthians 4 is that while our fragile bodies may be afflicted and perplexed and persecuted, we will not be destroyed. This is what Paul meant when he said that we are "always carrying in the body the death of Jesus, so that the life of Jesus may also be manifested in our bodies" (4:10). Our bodies are wearing down in illness, exhaustion, and persecution. But while we suffer, we are not overtaken to eternal death. Afflicted, yes, but we are not crushed. Life is perplexing and we are confused, but we do not live in despair. We may be persecuted, but we will never be forsaken. We are struck down, but never destroyed (4:9).

We can say with Paul:

> We do not lose heart. Though our outer self is wasting away, our inner self is being renewed day by day. For this light momentary affliction is preparing for us an eternal weight of glory beyond all comparison, as we look not to the things that are seen but to the things that are unseen. For the things that are seen are transient, but the things that are unseen are eternal. (2 Cor. 4:16–18)

When we have this eternal perspective, the power of God is revealed through us. We may struggle with pain and depression, but we can press on in faith because we know God will never let us go. And in the future God's resurrection power will finally deliver us from death. God's power is sufficient. These jars of clay will not forever break.[4]

Glory in Your Weakness for God's Glory

It sounds like a paradox, but it is a privilege to boast in our weaknesses because they reveal who our Father really is—a great God. One of my favorite examples of this is Gloria's reaction to adversity while she was in college. In her last year of studies she suffered a horrific eye injury. She was working at a construction site on a mission trip, and a nail mishit by a carpenter pierced her right eye. It left her blind in the eye until a major surgery restored much of her sight and saved the eye. It was actually a medical miracle that she didn't lose the eye because the nail miraculously swerved around her optic nerve in ways doctors can't explain. Apparently her story exists in a medical journal somewhere in a dusty library basement.

One of the best evangelistic opportunities Gloria ever had was walking around with a pirate patch telling people about Jesus. Her reaction to the injury and perseverance in trial was a bright light for the gospel. And she later glorified God in her weakness by putting a picture of the inside of her eye on the wall of her university campus office. That picture captured everyone's attention when they walked into her office, and Gloria had a clear opportunity to talk to people about her hope in God. She didn't waste her weakness.

Our response to pain and suffering can be a powerful evangelistic witness to the watching world. Have you ever considered that? Your weakness is a part of God's glorious plan for your life. I'm always inspired when I hear J. I. Packer talk about his childhood accident on the road that left a hole in his head and an indention in his skull for the rest of his life. This horrific injury as a seven-year-old changed his life forever. Then later in his youth he began to grasp God's work in weakness. Packer writes of this trial:

> My own recognition that the Christian way of life and service is a walk of weakness, as human strength gives out and only divine strength can sustain and enable, may well be rooted in my youth. A solitary and rather somber child, I had to wear at school, for ten years, a black aluminum patch covering a hole in my head, the result of a road accident, and hence I was unable to play outdoor games. During those years I felt out of most of what mattered, which is of course one form of the feeling of weakness.[5]

For Packer, God's sovereignty in his own weakness began to take root in his heart. He spent three weeks in the hospital and another six months in rehabilitation. Already a loner, when he went back to school with his patch, he secluded himself from others even more. He missed out on many things that "normal" children would experience. On his eleventh birthday he desperately wanted a bicycle just like other kids would receive around that age. On that special day he headed downstairs eagerly anticipating a set of wheels, only to find an old typewriter instead. Because his parents knew that one fall from a bicycle could prove deadly, they bought something else they thought he might learn to enjoy. The typewriter was old but in good condition. Packer was grieved at the sight of his gift. However, disappointment quickly turned into delight as soon as Packer began to type. The typewriter would later prove to be his most treasured possession. All his life, he never graduated to a computer but has always used a typewriter to write.[6]

Because J. I. Packer was disabled and weak, he could not receive the bicycle he desperately wanted, and instead his parents gave him a typewriter. What has God done through J. I. Packer over these years? Packer has been one of the most influential Christian theologians and writers of our time. Some thought that Packer might have brain damage after his accident, but instead God used that injury and enabled Packer to use his brain in ways that seven-year-old boy could never have dreamed. Rather than wallowing in self-pity at what he could not do, Packer, with a dent in his head, used that same mind to glorify God. God used his weakness to glorify himself.

The Glory of Jesus's Broken Body

God's power being made perfect in weakness is most perfectly displayed in the cross. In Revelation, when John catches a glimpse of heavenly glory and sees Jesus risen from the dead, the marks on his hands and feet are magnificently visible: "I saw a Lamb standing, as though it had been slain . . . and he went and took the scroll from the right hand of him who was seated on the throne" (Rev. 5:6–7). Jesus was and is the sacrificial Lamb slain for our sins. These marks are not a deformity, they are not a result of an accident or a defeat. They are the most beautiful scars in all of history. Jesus's broken body is our only hope and salvation. Now it is our privilege to point to Jesus through *our* scars. Our broken bodies can be a beautiful picture of God's glorious redemption.

Similar to the Japanese art of *Kintsugi*, our rough edges and cracks are filled in with gold to point to the greatness of God. The philosophy behind the art is not to build a new piece but instead to understand its history and repair the old piece. It looks similar to the old form but is now more glorious. This is what God does in our trials. We can embrace God in our suffering with faith that God is doing a work in us beyond our comprehension. Our scars are not things to run from or to hide from others. Through them we exalt the one who is conforming us more and more into the image of Christ. Paul points us to this reality as he closes his second letter to the Corinthians:

> So to keep me from becoming conceited because of the surpassing greatness of the revelations, a thorn was given me in the flesh, a messenger of Satan to harass me, to keep me from becoming conceited. Three times I pleaded with the Lord about this, that it should leave me. But he said to me, "My grace is sufficient for you, for my power is made perfect in weakness." Therefore I will boast all the more gladly of my weaknesses, so that the power of Christ may rest upon me. For the sake of Christ, then, I am content with weaknesses, insults, hardships, persecutions, and calamities. For when I am weak, then I am strong. (2 Cor. 12:7–10)

The apostle Paul, the greatest church planter of his time, constantly struggled with brokenness and trials of many kinds. It was his everyday life. He had some kind of "thorn" in the flesh that he often asked God to spare him from. We might wonder what Paul could have accomplished if he didn't have that thorn. But the reality is, everything Paul accomplished was done by God—not in spite of the thorn but through the thorn. The gospel was preached and churches planted not in spite of Paul's weakness but through his weakness.

Hurting friend, hope in the God who uses the weak. This doesn't make our suffering trite or easy. It is difficult. I hate my pain. Right now I sit slowly typing these words in agony because a ball struck my elbow at my daughter's soccer tournament yesterday. Just a few minutes ago my son brought me some Legos he desperately wanted me to disconnect for him. He struggles to grasp my disability and could not understand why Dad would not help him. There is nothing good about pain itself. But I know God will use my adversity in ways I cannot see right now. If only we could jump ahead ten or fifty years or into eternity and see all that God will do.

Friend, trust God—he will do more than you can envision in the dark moments. When we are frail and faint, let's boast more gladly in our weaknesses so that God's power may be made manifest in us. Let us be content in our circumstances, knowing that when we are weak, then we are strong.

10

YOU ARE A PART OF CHRIST'S BODY

The selfie stick has taken over the world. What few realize is that all owners of selfie sticks will be found out on the last day. OK, I'm joking. Mostly. I actually like selfies as much as the next amateur photographer, and I think selfie sticks are great. They are certainly an improvement on regular selfies that are so close up they tend to cut off my hair and make me look balder than I really am.

Of course, selfies sometimes go remarkably bad. I read about a man who took a selfie with a hijacker on a plane from Egypt. Let's just say that picture didn't go over well on social media. One time I witnessed a woman taking a selfie with a pile of dead sharks at the fish market. (Of course, I had to take a picture of her taking a picture of herself with the sharks.) Selfies are here, there, and everywhere. Selfies and selfie sticks are here to stay.

While selfies are great, they emphasize the self. We take pictures of ourselves at interesting places. We pose with celebrities and famous people. We photograph ourselves with our friends. We are the centers of our selfie universes. It's all about us. But the truth is, we are not meant to be the focal point of our lives. We are image bearers of God, made to reflect his glory—not our lesser selves. And further, as Christians, we are saved to image Christ and are made to be part of his body—the church.

God has always planned that his church would be the focal point of his work in this world. You may feel lonely or misunderstood. You may feel like your life has no meaning and your trials are overcoming you, but the good news is that there is more to this life for a believer. There is more to our lives than phones full of selfies, because we are a part of Christ's body where he is the center. That is good news for our weary hearts.

The Body of Christ

In his first letter to the Corinthians, Paul uses the analogy of a body to describe the church. He writes:

> For just as the body is one and has many members, and all the members of the body, though many, are one body, so it is with Christ. For in one Spirit we were all baptized into one body—Jews or Greeks, slaves or free—and all were made to drink of one Spirit.
>
> For the body does not consist of one member but of many. If the foot should say, "Because I am not a hand, I do not belong to the body," that would not make it any less a part of the body. And if the ear should say,

> "Because I am not an eye, I do not belong to the body," that would not make it any less a part of the body. If the whole body were an eye, where would be the sense of hearing? If the whole body were an ear, where would be the sense of smell? But as it is, God arranged the members in the body, each one of them, as he chose. If all were a single member, where would the body be? As it is, there are many parts, yet one body. (1 Cor. 12:12–20)

Paul's point is that all believers are part of one body. Spiritually speaking, you are actually closer with a Christian who is a stranger to you than you are with an unbelieving family member. You are bonded with that other believer in Christ and have been saved not in isolation from other believers, but you have been saved into Christ's body. We were made for something more than selfies.

This means that all Christians are a part of the body, even hurting Christians. Regardless of your health or capacity, if you are a believer, then you are a part of the body. If you are healthy, you are a part of the body. But if you are broken, depressed, and hurting, you are a part of that same body of Christ. No disease or disorder casts you outside the body. No sickness keeps you from playing a part.

The Church Needs You

For the body of Christ to be healthy we must depend on each part of the body. The church at Corinth seems to have demoralized those members whom they assumed were less gifted or hurting. Perhaps some of those struggling wondered whether they should even be regarded as part of the church body. Those of us who are hurting are reassured that the body has need of *every* part.

Every part must play its role, or the body won't function as well as it could. It would be ridiculous if our whole body were one nose. Not only would it be gross but it also couldn't walk or talk. Every one of us is different, and that's a good thing. We are not all good at the same things. In the sport of cricket, the best bowlers are not any more valuable than the best batsman. In baseball you need both hitters and pitchers to have a successful team. In both sports the fielders have to play well. All have a part to play.

This is why we continue being in community with God's people all the days of our lives. When one part of the body leaves the body, the whole body hurts. The church *needs* you! Individual members cannot contract out the work; they must do their role for the good of the body.[1] Romans 12:5 says, "So we, though many, are one body in Christ, and individually members one of another." Christianity is not a spectator sport. We don't stay in the seats and watch other Christians get in the match. A few years ago I watched all-time tennis greats Roger Federer and Rafael Nadal on television play in the Australian Open final. I knew it was probably the last time these two tennis greats would play each other. It was incredible to watch these two rivals. But nothing compares with actually playing the game yourself. Watching is fun, but nothing beats getting out on the court and playing your best.

You may feel as if you have nothing to give others—you are in so much pain, your trial is tremendous. You get exhausted by just getting yourself ready in the morning. But one of the best things you can do as you struggle in your trials is to serve others. This is what you were made to do.

God made you to play your part. You were not an accident. In 1 Corinthians 12:18, we see that "God arranged the members in the body." He put them together. God makes no mistakes; he created you just the way he wanted to. There was no casualty in creation.[2] You may not feel as if you can serve in the way you would like to, but you are important to the health of the church. Sam Allberry gives this illustration in his book on the church:

> Take a pen, a piece of paper and a timer. How many times can you write your name in 30 seconds? Now try the same exercise but without using your hands. You can put the pen between your toes or hold it in your mouth. My guess is, you didn't do so well the second time round. Once you remove certain parts of the body, even simple tasks get harder. It reminds us of how much those with disability deserve our admiration. And it also reminds us of what our church misses out on when we are not there—part of the body is missing. Your church needs you.[3]

When you reject Christ's body, the whole church loses something. We need each other, and the wonderful fact is that the Lord has uniquely made you and can use you not in spite of your circumstances but *because* of your circumstances. This is a wonderful truth!

I've noticed that my nerve pain has given me a unique experience with chronic pain and disability that has allowed me to speak into people's lives in profound ways. I had very little sympathy for others before I myself needed sympathy. Now I understand (at least a little bit more than I used to) the physical and emotional pain that comes with failing health. But what if I steered clear of the rest of Christ's body? What if I saw my trial as a parenthesis or break in my church involvement and distanced myself from God's people for a time? I would miss out on God using me. Hurting friend, God can use you in extraordinary ways. God has sovereignly ordained to use hurting people to comfort other hurting people. Paul writes:

> Blessed be the God and Father of our Lord Jesus Christ, the Father of mercies and God of all comfort, who comforts us in all our affliction, so that we may be able to comfort those who are in any affliction, with the comfort with which we ourselves are comforted by God. (2 Cor. 1:3–4)

Being unhealthy or struggling with some trial shouldn't cause you to stop your church involvement. You shouldn't think that you'll get involved once you're healthy. The church needs you now. I love how one of our former church members, Sneha, deals with extreme physical pain and yet works hard to join her new church for corporate worship even when she doesn't feel well. Sneha understands that she needs the church now more than ever. And she's a blessing to all. Even when she's writhing in pain in her apartment, she will call fellow church members to encourage and pray for them. Ladies will come to her apartment so that she can teach them the Bible. That's what Paul is talking about when he says God comforts us so we can comfort others. The reassuring thing for those who are hurting is that God doesn't cast us aside in our trials, but he is actually preparing us to be used in ways beyond what we could even imagine. Paul continues:

> The eye cannot say to the hand, "I have no need of you," nor again the head to the feet, "I have no need of you." On the contrary, the parts of the body that seem to be weaker are indispensable, and on those parts of the body that we think less honorable we bestow the greater honor, and our unpresentable parts are treated with greater modesty, which our more presentable parts do not require. But God has so composed the body, giving greater honor to the part that lacked it, that there may be no division in the body, but that the members may have the same care for one another. If one member suffers, all suffer together; if one member is honored, all rejoice together. (1 Cor. 12:21–26)

This is great news! Even when we are hurting and we may be weaker than the other parts, God uses us. Even when we may feel like we have nothing to give, what does Paul say to us? He says *all* parts are indispensable. Hurting friend, you are indispensable in the plan of God! The word *weaker* in this context actually has the idea of being sick.[4] The meaning emphasizes the complete unimportance of the member. But Paul says, "We need those members!" The body of Christ can't do without them.[5] Paul writes that those parts actually deserve greater honor. It seems counterintuitive, but in God's grand design, your trial might be the moment of your most significant ministry. Could that be the case in your life right now?

You Need the Church

Being a part of Christ's body means we have the privilege of gathering with our fellow brothers and sisters in Christ for worship each week. The author of Hebrews writes, "Let us consider how to stir up one another to love and good works, not neglecting to meet together, as is the habit of some, but encouraging one another, and all the more as you see the Day drawing near" (Heb. 10:24–25). When we come together, we remind each other that Jesus is our Savior. We can do this anytime we meet with another believer, but one of the strongest ways to do this is by worshiping together weekly as a congregation. Corporate worship is a bit like watching the television show *Monk*. Watching *Monk* isn't like watching a sporting event, where you don't know if your team is going to win. Adrian Monk, the world's greatest detective, always, always catches the culprit. It's as good as done even while the opening credits are still rolling. When you start an episode of *Monk*, you are not wondering if he's going to catch the bad guy and win. You watch the show because it's exciting to see how he's going to win this time around.[6]

Similarly (but obviously a bit differently), when you are with God's people on a weekly basis, you are not wondering if Jesus is going to win and defeat evil. You don't go to the church service to find out if Jesus is victorious in that day's portion of Scripture. You know he is! You know he wins, but you go each week to be with God's people and recount again and again together that Jesus has already paid it all and won eternity for us. It is finished. And so we read and pray through biblical truth together. We sing to one another and to God and hear the Word preached. Baptism and the Lord's Supper point to the cosmic victory that Jesus has won for us. It's like a shot of grace to our hearts when we gather with other members of the body and are reminded together of this good news. We can never get enough of Jesus together. Realizing that we are a part of Christ's greater body and worshiping together with the other members is a grand privilege!

The body of Christ also helps us fight sin and see ourselves more accurately. It's really hard to see ourselves like others do. For instance, I cringe at the sound of my own voice on a sermon recording. It sounds much too high and awkward. I suppose this is because when I hear myself speak, I'm too close to hear what I really sound like. I'm hearing it from a different vantage point than everyone else. As I'm talking, I think I sound like Morgan Freeman, but later when listening to a recording of myself it sounds more like a whiny and annoying person from outer space. I think to myself, "There is no way I sound like that!" But my friends, and certainly my wife, assure me that's exactly what I sound like.[7]

I wish it were just my voice that I perceive wrongly. I am ignorant of many other things too. I was thankful when a fellow pastor at our church took some time to speak into my life and let me know how others perceived some of my outward actions. One of the blessings of being a part of the body is that when one body part needs to be rebuked, other members can step up and speak into our hearts.

The other members of the body are also there to bear one another's burdens in times of trial. It is especially sweet when other believers' lives get so intertwined with your life that they begin carrying the weight of your pain upon them. I have been encouraged over the years when many of my fellow members have given me rides to church events or accompanied me to a birthday party or small group meeting.

I have been supported by friends and staff members who have taken time away from their families to travel with me around the world. I have countless examples of moments when in the midst of heightened pain and disappointment a fellow elder stopped whatever it is we were doing, laid a hand on my shoulder, and prayed for me. I need the church.

I recently came across a video of four blind men competing in the 100-meter sprint finals in the Paralympics. I wish the Paralympics received more attention than the Olympics, because it's wonderful to see people overcome physical disability to do extraordinary things. In this particular video, each of the four men ran with a guide. It was the only way they could get to the finish line. The guides got them set on the blocks and then ran beside them the whole race. They ran so close together they were just about holding hands. It was breathtaking to watch.

These blind athletes train with their guides all year long. They travel together to competitions. They eat together, run together, and do everything together. The guides need to be just as fast as the runners because they run side by side. In the same way, we need people in our lives who are with us each step of the way. If we try to run alone in our trials, we'll be like a blind man trying to run a race without a guide. We'll trip up and fall. We can't live our lives by ourselves.

What a joyful thought that a Christian is never alone. We are in Christ and placed in Christ's body. There is always a place for us at the table with other believers—all beautiful and all with a role to play.

11

CHRIST WILL HOLD YOU FAST

We have all lost something important to us. Some of us have lost friends we've failed to keep up with. We've lost important documents or misplaced our wallet. We might lose our keys, our baseball tickets, or a file on our computer. A few of us even lose our phone . . . every day. I won't name names.

While on a date at a Dubai mall years ago, Gloria and I lost our car. We thought it was stolen as we searched the mall parking garage for over an hour. Only later did we realize we were simply on the wrong level. But that was nothing compared to the time we lost our car in Spain. We were with a short-term outreach team and had parked our car in downtown Málaga. After eating dinner with the team, we walked out to the car, but it wasn't where we thought it should be. We looked around and asked everyone we could. Each person sent us to another person and then another. Eventually we visited a police department who then sent us to another police office.

We were so sure that the city was playing a practical joke on us!

Eventually the police sent us on what felt like a scavenger car hunt to the other side of the city. And there we found our car— clear across town in a portion of a parking garage that looked like car prison. Our vehicle was literally in a car jail cell. Apparently we had parked somewhere we shouldn't have, and the car had been towed away. We were expecting a huge fine, but we simply paid a few euros and purchased a normal parking ticket. We rescued our vehicle and arrived at our hotel safe and sound just after 3 a.m. Apparently losing cars is not too hard to do (at least for my wife and me).

You probably have similar stories about losing valuable things. Hurting friend, I want to focus on a truth that has held me tight in the dark nights of my soul: God never loses us.

The Inheritance

In 1 Peter 1 the apostle directs our hearts and minds to this diamond of a truth. Peter writes:

> Blessed be the God and Father of our Lord Jesus Christ! According to his great mercy, he has caused us to be born again to a living hope through the resurrection of Jesus Christ from the dead, to an inheritance that is imperishable, undefiled, and unfading, kept in heaven for you. (1 Pet. 1:3–4)

God will never lose you. He will never, ever, ever lose you. This a breathtaking truth.

Peter is not speaking of an earthly inheritance that parents pass down to children. He is not talking about an estate or a fancy gold necklace. These inheritances often get lost or damaged. Peter doesn't tell us exactly what the inheritance will be, but he describes it as imperishable. It's unable to decay. It's indestructible. It's also undefiled, unable to be stained or ruined. And it's unfading. This inheritance can't lose its value like an earthly estate might. It's not subject to the volatile ups and downs of the stock market or the shrewdness of our investing strategies. It will never lose its value because God himself is keeping it for us in heaven.

The Bible also shows us specifically how God keeps this inheritance for us:

> In him you also, when you heard the word of truth, the gospel of your salvation, and believed in him, were sealed with the promised Holy Spirit, who is the guarantee of our inheritance until we acquire possession of it, to the praise of his glory. (Eph. 1:13–14)

The Spirit does at least two things after we believe in Christ. First, we are sealed with the Holy Spirit. This is the image of a king sealing a royal document by pressing his signet ring into wax, leaving his impression of royal authority. In a way, the Spirit is the signet ring of our triune God. He makes a mark on our souls, showing God's ownership of us. A seal can describe protection against outsiders. You seal your house and lock it up before leaving for vacation. You seal your envelope before putting it in the mail. Christians are sealed by God against the Devil and his schemes. We are protected by the King.[1]

Second, the Spirit is the guarantee of our inheritance. The term *guarantee* comes from commercial and business language. It's similar to the idea of a deposit. You might pay a deposit when you purchase a home. You sign the contract and leave a guarantee to show your intention to pay everything you owe for the home. It's a pledge or a promise. But while there are times when we may fail on our promises, the Holy Spirit never reneges on his promises. God is unable to go back on his word. He promises to finish what he has begun. This heavenly inheritance is guaranteed.[2]

The Perseverance of the Savior

If you're a child of God, you can be sure that he will keep you to the end because he will do it through his strength, not yours. The very next verse in 1 Peter 1 tells us that we "by God's power are being guarded through faith for a salvation ready to be revealed in the last time" (1 Pet. 1:5).

Even as you endure the most horrible pain imaginable, you are being held together through God's power and guarded by him. The word *guarded* can be translated "protected." It is the word used to describe the construction of garrisons in a city to protect it from its enemies.[3] This is what God is doing for all believers. He has put a wall of defense around each of our lives and is guarding our salvation. He is protecting our faith with the best defense system in the universe. It has a perfect success rate. He has never lost one of his heirs.

It is incredibly encouraging that we persevere because of God. You might feel utterly powerless in your affliction. You may think you don't have the strength to hold on to your faith. You can hardly make it through a day keeping yourself together. The crushing power of your trial leaves you without stamina to keep fighting. You are depressed and lonely. You are broken and sense that you're losing your grip on life and there is no way you can endure any longer. But friend, God won't lose you! Some theologians call this doctrine "the perseverance of the saints," but R. C. Sproul always said that this doctrine could better be called the "*preservation* of the saints."[4] Sproul was saying that we don't persevere in our own strength, but God preserves us in his strength. It's really the perseverance of the Savior. God won't stop short of bringing his children home.

We are being guarded through faith, by God's power. Even our faith is from God. It is a gift. Some of you are struggling through tough times and thinking, "I don't know if I can hold on to God." In the midst of your trials don't miss that he's holding on to you. The same God who keeps our inheritance also keeps *us* for our inheritance. Our church's statement of faith says this about believers: "A special providence watches over their welfare and they are kept by the power of God through faith unto salvation." In a special providence of God we are protected until the fullness of our salvation is revealed at the end. He will have this salvation ready. We can do nothing to prepare it. There is no need for us to come alongside God as consultants in designing it. Disease and depression don't render us disqualified. Persecution and even martyrdom won't separate us from God. No sickness, no evil, no injustice, and no pain can keep us from God. Romans 8 asks a poignant question and gives a stunning answer:

> Who shall separate us from the love of Christ? Shall tribulation, or distress, or persecution, or famine, or nakedness, or danger, or sword? . . . For I am sure that neither death nor life, nor angels nor rulers, nor things present nor things to come, nor powers, nor height nor depth, nor anything else in all creation, will be able to

> separate us from the love of God in Christ Jesus our Lord. (Rom. 8:35, 38-39)

Nothing can separate us from the love of Christ. Nothing. Our hope is grounded in the past (Christ's death and resurrection) and assured in the future (our undefiled inheritance), which gives us hope in the present.

Jesus Is Our Only Hope

If you feel like you're barely holding on, there is hope. If you feel like you're stumbling through a never-ending cave of darkness, there is good news. If you've repented of your sin and believed in Jesus for your salvation, then God will never let you go. You are right to doubt yourself. You are right to say you are unworthy of God's love for you. You are right to say you can't do it. You are right to say you can't keep yourself saved. You and I *are* unworthy, and we can't do it. You did nothing to earn your salvation, and you can do nothing to keep yourself saved. And you can do nothing to make God let go of you. Your salvation is a gift you've been given. You can't give it back. And no one can take it away. Jesus says, "My sheep hear my voice, and I know them, and they follow me. I give them eternal life, and they will never perish, and no one will snatch them out of my hand" (John 10:27–28).

No one can take you from God. Hold on to faith. Perhaps you have turned to the world to satisfy your desires in the midst of your pain. When pain is severe, it is tempting to turn to alcohol, pornography, bitterness, or other mind-numbing realities to try to subdue the torment. Sin is the great enemy of assurance.[5] You may have delved into sin beyond anything you have dug into before. You may even wonder if it is possible for a real Christian to do such things. Friend, flee to Christ in confession and repentance. Find solace in the Savior.

We can't lose our salvation, but we also don't sit back and just let go and let God. God's perseverance of us doesn't mean we can go on sinning (Rom. 6:1–2). If we are born again in Christ, our nature is changed and we live to please God. We are people of repentance. But this doesn't mean that we sin no more. There will be moments where we have to turn back to God and repent of our sin. We can be confident that he will forgive us and that our sin will not disqualify us from salvation. As Milton Vincent writes:

> The gospel also reminds me that my righteous standing with God always holds firm regardless of my performance, because my standing is based solely on the work of Jesus and not mine. On my worst days of sin and failure, the gospel encourages me with God's unrelenting grace toward me. On my best days of victory and usefulness, the gospel keeps me relating to God solely on the basis of Jesus' righteousness and not mine.[6]

God is holding on to us, but we need to hold on to him in response.

Paul sent Timothy to the Thessalonians with a letter because Paul was worried about them. He says, "For this reason, when I could bear it no longer, I sent to learn about your faith, for fear that somehow the tempter had tempted you and our labor would be in vain" (1 Thess. 3:5).

He was concerned that these believers would abandon their faith because of their trials. They were being persecuted, and Paul feared that Satan was disturbing their work with the church and that they were turning away from Christ. Paul didn't assume they were truly believers just because they positively received the message by faith when Paul first preached to them. The validity of their faith was shown in how they responded to trials, so their persistence in that same faith in Christ was the proof that it was genuine.[7] If you are believing in Christ in the midst of your pain, friend, be encouraged: that's the proof that God will keep you to the end.

Even when your faith seems weak and barely present, be encouraged. I remember those dark nights of the soul when we first moved to the Middle East. There in the village our whole world was falling apart. I hated my life. Lightning bolts of nerve pain made it feel like the bones in my arms were on fire. At times I would sit on the couch and just stare off into nothing for hours on end. I wanted to give up. It felt like each day did further destruction to my soul, and my faith was hanging on by a thread. But it was there.

Tim Keller has often said that it's not the strength of our faith that is the most important thing. Weak faith is still faith. He writes:

> Imagine you are on a high cliff and you lose your footing and begin to fall. Just beside you is a branch sticking out of the edge of the cliff. It is your only hope and seems more than strong enough. How can it save you? If you're certain the branch can support you, but you don't actually reach out and grab it, you are lost. If instead your mind is filled with doubts and uncertainty that the branch can hold you, but you reach out and grab it anyway, you will be saved. Why? It is not the

> strength of your faith but the object of your faith that actually saves you. Strong faith in a weak branch is fatally inferior to weak faith in a strong branch.[8]

What matters is the object of our faith. Our God is trustworthy. He doesn't lose us like we lose our keys or even our cars. He doesn't misplace or lose track of us. He doesn't regret ever knowing us in the first place. Look to Christ—he will hold you to the end.

12

EXTREME MAKEOVER

At times I have wished I didn't have my arms. I have even dreamed that I didn't have any arms at all. I have pain every single moment of every single day. On the worst nights I am writhing in pain as I turn from side to side trying my hardest to get comfortable and fall asleep. At work I sometimes can't think straight because of the throbbing nerve endings around my elbows and hands. As soon as the alarm sounds to wake me up in the morning, I have to discipline myself not to meditate on all the reasons I have to hate the fact that my arms are broken.

But it's not just the physical pain that threatens to undo me. There is also emotional distress that accompanies my condition. I have regular social anxiety when I meet new people, which, for a pastor, happens about every three seconds.

Upon each greeting I have to explain to new acquaintances why I am unable to shake their hand, while trying to avoid a friendly hand squeeze or elbow grab. This naturally leads into sharing how I'm not germaphobic (though I sort of am) but disabled. Not only do I want to avoid having my hands or arms injured when greeting someone, but I also want to avoid needlessly offending that person.

Because there are no wheelchairs for those with arm disabilities, my handicap isn't easy to spot at first glance and an explanation is almost always expected by every person I meet. This social anxiety makes it hard for me to get excited about going to a conference or another event where I'll have to face this reality a hundred times.

Perhaps the worst emotional strain is the hopeless feeling that floods my heart as I try to play with my children. I love sports and always dreamed of playing with my kids. I relive the pain of that shattered dream every time I'm reminded that I can't play catch with my kids the way I'd like to. My oldest son, Judson, recently received a couple of rackets to play badminton, and he was giddy with excitement to play with me. And then all of a sudden it dawned on him. As he walked up to me, he paused in the middle of his invitation and was reminded that I couldn't actually play the new game with him. I'm sure both of our hearts sank a little bit in that moment. It was crushing to my soul. I wanted more than anything to pick up that racket and play with him. Unfortunately there's no way to will your body to do things it just can't do. Oh how I wish my body were different!

Your life is probably different from mine, yet there may be many similarities. Your body and mind are likely not what you want them to be. Maybe you have a physical disability or are battling depression. Or perhaps it's a trial that you hope will pass but the agony is unbearable today. You know full well the truth that our bodies and minds on this earth are frail and fraught with weakness.

Thankfully this isn't the final chapter for our bodies. A more permanent home awaits, and this is good news I have to remind myself of every single day.

A Permanent Home

Right now, our bodies and minds decay, but a permanent home awaits.

Paul writes:

> For we know that if the tent that is our earthly home is destroyed, we have a building from God, a house not made with hands, eternal in the heavens. For in this tent we groan, longing to put on our heavenly dwelling, if indeed by putting it on we may not be found naked. For while we are still in this tent, we groan, being burdened—not that we would be unclothed, but that we would be further clothed, so that what is mortal may be swallowed up by life. He who has prepared us for this very thing is God, who has given us the Spirit as a guarantee. (2 Cor. 5:1–5)

It's not surprising that Paul, a tentmaker by trade, compares our earthly bodies to tents.[1] I don't own a tent, but I used one on a couple camping trips as a child. I think the worst thing about camping may be the actual tent itself. I easily get claustrophobic. When the rain falls, you can hear it hitting the tent just inches from your face. And the worst thing is the buzzing of mosquitos next to your face, making you feel like they are feasting on your flesh all night long. That's because they probably are! As you can see, sleeping on a hard floor inside a shabby tent isn't too compelling for me.

A tent is a temporary dwelling place, not a permanent residence. In 2 Corinthians Paul paints a picture of the better, more glorious body as a *house* in comparison to a *tent*. Today, Paul says, we live in a tent, but a day is coming when our bodies will be more like a house. Tents break and often need to be replaced. They hardly protect you from high and low temperatures and precipitation. A house is sturdy and provides shelter from the elements. A house is also comfortable and makes you feel at home. There is something wonderful about coming back from a long trip and opening the front door to your house and stepping back in. In that moment all seems right in the world.

In this life, our bodies face disease and decay. Paul says, "For in this tent we groan, longing to put on our heavenly dwelling" (2 Cor. 5:2).

We ache for the permanent and more glorious stability of a new home. And it's coming! J. I. Packer writes:

> Second Corinthians 5:1–8 sets before us in picture language that aspect of our hope which will counter, cancel, and consign to far-off memory "this light momentary affliction"—the bad health, crippled limbs, bodily pains; minds, memories, relationships, personal circumstances all going downhill; insults, cruelties, and whatever else. This hope fills us with wondering joy that everything can be so good. We shall be given a new dwelling place, says Paul, new clothes,

> and a new home life in the company of our Lord. It sounds marvelous, and so indeed it is. It sounds, in fact, too good to be true, but that is not the case.[2]

We will one day move on from the tent of this earthly body and have a heavenly home, and it will indeed be marvelous.

A Better Body

We don't know exactly what our bodies will be like in heaven, but we do know they will be glorious. Philippians 3:20–21 says, "But our citizenship is in heaven, and from it we await a Savior, the Lord Jesus Christ, who will transform our lowly body to be like his glorious body, by the power that enables him even to subject all things to himself." Philippi was a Roman colony governed by the laws of Rome. Unlike most conquered regions of the empire, the citizens wore Roman clothes, and they were proud to be a part of the empire. Paul tells the church that while this earthly citizenship made them proud, it's temporary, and their permanent passport has heaven written all over it. We were made for heaven, and our bodies in glory will be of a different nature than here on earth. Jesus will transform our lowly body, which literally means, "the body of our humiliation." In contrast to our new body, this one is almost embarrassing. In making this comparison, Paul is addressing the limitation of our bodies here on earth.[3] Our new body will be more suited for the heavenly realm. And our new body won't just be better—it will actually be like Christ's glorious body.

This blows my mind. By the power of Jesus, our fallen bodies will become like his glorified heavenly body. Those of us with chronic pain, fatigue, or disability, and even those who are facing the normal limitations of old age can hope that Jesus will transform our "humiliating" body to be like his resurrection body. It will be like a remarkable alteration, like a seed growing into its own characteristic flower.[4] Alec Motyer says, "A seed is a humble thing, unprepossessing and to all outward appearance unpromising. Yet this seed becomes that flower in a continuous process of wonderful transformation."[5] A seed blossoms into a flower when its glory is fully realized.

First Corinthians 15 speaks of the transformation that will happen to our bodies:

> But someone will ask, "How are the dead raised? With what kind of body do they come?" You foolish person! What you sow does not come to life unless it dies. And what you sow is not the body that is to be, but a bare kernel, perhaps of wheat or of some other grain. But God gives it a body as he has chosen, and to each kind of seed its own body. (1 Cor. 15:35–38)

There was likely an objection in the Corinthian church that went something like this: "We're supposed to get a better body, but it sounds like it will only get worse. Our bodies are flawed on this earth, and after we die, they are buried and only corrupt more. A rotten body is a worse body! How is this going to work?" Paul counters the argument by pointing to the miracle of the harvest. The seed is buried in the ground, but later is raised out of the ground to a more glorious reality.[6] While our bodies are sown in corruption, dishonor, and weakness, they will be raised in incorruption and glory and power. Just as God made our bodies perfectly for life on earth when he created us, so he will make our bodies perfect for life in heaven.[7]

It's a wonderful thought that our bodies will be raised from the dead. This implies that we will not be given a completely new body but that our current body will be transformed. This must be the case, otherwise Paul would never have said that the seed would have to die before it grows into its final state. This is a thrilling thought for those of us who are disabled. A day is coming when our bodies will not only work and be without pain, but our bodies will be utterly transformed. Packer writes:

> Our new body, we may be sure, will match and perfectly express our perfected new heart, that is, our renewed moral and spiritual nature and character. That body will reflect us as we were at our best, rather than as we are physically at the time of leaving this world; indeed, we should expect it to be better than our physical best ever was. The new body will never deteriorate, but will keep its newness for all eternity. It will know no inner tensions between one desire and another, each pulling against the other, nor will desire to do something ever outrun energy and ability to do it. Nor, when we are in glory, shall we ever lack, or fail to show, love to the Father, the Son, and the Holy Spirit, and to all the brothers and sisters in Christ who are with us there.[8]

The humility of the seed will turn into a flower in blossom. There will be no more pain.

Hope for the Future

The Scriptures are filled with truths about our new bodies too wonderful to comprehend. Our new bodies will not have any disabilities (Isa. 35:3–5). Our bodies will be changed instantly when we are raised (1 Cor. 15:51–53). Our new body will reflect Christ's glory (2 Cor. 3:17–18).

This gives us hope as our bodies waste away in this life. The apostle Paul wrestled with bodily affliction, though he did not lose hope. He wrote: "So we do not lose heart. Though our outer self is wasting away, our inner self is being renewed day by day" (2 Cor. 4:16). Paul was able to encourage himself with the truth of his future body even as he was suffering. John Piper says of the aging apostle who wrote 2 Corinthians:

> He [Paul] can't see the way he used to (and there were no glasses). He can't hear the way he used to (and there were no hearing aids). He doesn't recover from beatings the way he used to (and there were no antibiotics). His strength, walking from town to town, doesn't hold up the way it used to. He sees the wrinkles in his face and neck. His memory is not as good. His joints get stiff when he sits still. He knows that he, like everyone else, is dying. And he admits that this is a threat to his faith and joy and courage. But he doesn't lose heart. Why? . . . He doesn't lose heart because the inner man is being renewed. The renewing of the heart comes from something very strange: it comes from looking at what he can't see. . . . We look not to the things that are seen but to the things that are unseen. For the things that are seen are transient, but the

> things that are unseen are eternal. That's Paul's way of not losing heart: looking at what you can't see.[9]

Paul was fixing his eyes on future hope. He was setting the eyes of his heart on Jesus. While he couldn't see the Savior physically, his faith became his sight. Paul's reality was 2 Corinthians 4:17: "For this light momentary affliction is preparing for us an eternal weight of glory beyond all comparison." Paul was able to press on through the pain because he understood that his pain was not pointless. His pain had a profound purpose. It pointed him toward Christ. The suffering he endured was producing within him an eternal weight of glory far beyond all comparison.[10] The thought of the weight of glory exhilarated the apostle. Piper writes, "When he's hurting, he fixes his eyes not on how heavy the hurt is, but on how heavy the glory will be because of the hurt."[11] Our pain now is very little when compared to the weightiness, the heaviness of what's to come. They don't even compare. Our glorious bodies will be so much better than the bodies we have now that we can't even wrap our minds around it. Our present suffering is not imaginary, but it is temporary.

When my alarm rings in the morning, I need to fight to remind myself that today is not the end of the story. It may be a day filled with difficulty, but another chapter is coming, and it is too glorious to fathom. The glory of eternity far outweighs my struggles today.

Praise God.

13

HEAVEN IS FOR REAL

Walk into your average Christian bookstore around the world and you will quickly notice several things. You will almost always be greeted by warm and friendly employees who are ready to help you find what you need. You'll see sections of Bibles, Bible studies, books, and various trinkets. As you turn to the books, you'll see banners dividing up the sections. Quite often the largest display you'll see is filled with books on the subject of heaven. In some stores, this section is often waiting to greet you as soon as you come through the doors.

Many of these books are written by people who claim to have gone to heaven and then come back to earth. Many of the authors have had near-death experiences, where they claim they were in heaven for a short time but God told them their time on earth wasn't over and they had to go back. They wake up from surgery, a coma, or some other illness ready to tell their tale of the afterlife.

People line up to purchase these titles and even to watch the movies developed from the books. "Heaven tourism" books are big business and have sold millions of copies around the world.[1] This genre connects with our hearts because we desperately want to know what heaven is like. For those of us hurting, we yearn to know about the benefits of the next life. All of us to some extent look forward to feeling the comfort of eternity. It's the reason we are tempted to reach for heavenly book after heavenly book—we want a glimpse into this reality.

But there is only one book that gives us a clear picture of heaven. The author of one now-recalled heaven book wrote this as his motive for writing a false account: "I said I went to heaven because I thought it would get me attention. When I made the claims that I did, I had never read the Bible. People have profited from lies, and continue to. They should read the Bible, which is enough. The Bible is the only source of truth. Anything written by man cannot be infallible."[2] It sounds like this young man now understands the truth: the Bible gives us the clearest picture of heaven. For those of us who are hurting, we need to look at what God's Word says about the afterlife. The hope for a glorious tomorrow is the hope we need for today.

A New Hope

Revelation 21:1–4 says:

> Then I saw a new heaven and a new earth, for the first heaven and the first earth had passed away, and the sea was no more. And I saw the holy city, new Jerusalem, coming down out of heaven from God, prepared as a

> bride adorned for her husband. And I heard a loud voice from the throne saying, "Behold, the dwelling place of God is with man. He will dwell with them, and they will be his people, and God himself will be with them as their God. He will wipe away every tear from their eyes, and death shall be no more, neither shall there be mourning, nor crying, nor pain anymore, for the former things have passed away."

A new heaven and a new earth are coming. This is great news. The word for "new" here normally indicates a newness in terms of quality, not time. It's the idea that the first earth was imperfect and the second one will be more glorious in every way.[3] The new heavens and new earth will have identifiable parts just as the body will be raised without losing its former identity.[4] But there will be a newness that will be evident in every possible way.

This new and improved heaven and earth will also be fundamentally different from the old one. The new one has been prepared like a bride for her husband. On her wedding day a bride puts on a beautiful dress, has her hair styled and makeup done in an extravagant way, and does whatever she can to present herself to her groom at the altar in a most glorious state. It's a transformation, and she may very well look more radiant on that day than at any other point in her life. The new heaven and new earth will be more wonderful than anything we can see on this earth. We may see glimpses of that glory now, but they are merely shadows of the reality that is to come.

In this new heaven and new earth there will be no tears. God will wipe away every tear from our eyes (Rev. 21:4).

A day is coming when there will be no more cancer. Diseased elbows will bend. The lame will get up, walk, and dance with joy. The depressed will see their darkness lift and will sing of their never-ending gladness. The anxieties of the morning will be long gone. Our daily struggle with sin will be finished. The shame of being abused will be scorched. Worrying about death will be impossible because one day death will die. We won't worry about money, because everything will be supplied to us in Christ Jesus. Persecution will be impossible because we will all love God. God says, "Behold, I am making all things new" (Rev. 21:5).

I look forward to the day when I will no longer get stuck in airplane bathrooms because I don't have the strength to open the door. I eagerly anticipate a time when I won't need help buttoning my shirt and getting dressed for the day. One day I won't lie in bed at night writhing in pain unable to get rest. My ongoing battle with depression will be won. I won't suffer from social anxiety wondering how my disability will be perceived. And the tears that accompany all these things will be wiped away. Isn't this glorious?

The repeated prayer of the Old Testament saints was that God would reveal his presence by "shining the light of his countenance" on them.[5] This prayer is answered in Revelation 22:5, which says that in the new heaven and earth, "night will be no more." Instead the Son of God will be the sun, and his glory will light our way. The shining of God's face was equated with perseverance and peace for Christians.[6] This is why we named our first daughter Aliza Sahar, which means "joyful dawn." That first dawn of eternity will mark the end of darkness. It will be the most joyful morning because God himself will be a radiant light that will swallow the darkness forever.

We Will Be with Jesus

I love the thought of celebrating with my brothers and sisters in Christ at the marriage supper of the Lamb for all eternity. The closest comparison I have is an Amish buffet in Pennsylvania called Shady Maple Smorgasbord. There is only one word to describe this establishment: epic. Shady Maple has at least twenty different stations of food, four kinds of biscuits and gravy (my personal favorite), and eight ICEE machines—for breakfast! It is a culinary paradise.

The marriage supper will be even more wonderful than this, and we will be with all our fellow believers from all time. It will be incredible to be gathered together with long-lost loved ones and to be with heroes of the faith from past centuries. But while the fellowship will be incredible, we can't miss one of the most precious statements in all of Scripture: "They will see his face" (Rev. 22:4). The most amazing part about heaven is not what we will receive, but that we will be in the presence of our Savior. Heaven will be a place without pain, but the most assuring part of it will be that we will be face-to-face with King Jesus. That's the greatest part of eternal life. Heaven will be amazing because we will be with Jesus. We get to be with our great God.

The face of God was denied to Moses (Ex. 33:20, 23), but it is the privilege of all of God's servants in the holy city.[7] His name will be on our foreheads, attaching ourselves to the King forever (Rev. 22:4). G. K. Beale says that having his name on our foreheads intensifies the notion of intimate fellowship with God. He writes: “It is beyond coincidence that God’s name was written on the high priest’s forehead in the OT. This expresses further the priestly nature of God’s new people.”[8] We will all be priests forever in heaven, clearly marked by him and protected by his power.

The End Is Certain

My wife is a big fan of author J. R. R. Tolkien. She read many of his books as a child, and when The Lord of the Rings movies were released, she made me watch them with her multiple times. Soon I knew everything that would happen. I knew how the movies would end and how evil would be defeated.

Something similar has happened with Satan and his minions. The story has been written and the conclusion settled, however, it will be a rough ride to the end. Jesus has won and Satan has lost; but as someone once said, “The dragon has been slain, but his tail still swishes.”[9] Even though Satan is as good as dead, he still wreaks havoc in the world. This is why we can’t forget that the end will come. Jesus has conquered and will have ultimate victory.

> Who shall separate us from the love of Christ? Shall tribulation, or distress, or persecution, or famine, or nakedness, or danger, or sword? . . . For I am sure that neither death nor life, nor angels nor rulers, nor things present nor things to come, nor powers, nor height nor depth, nor anything else in all creation, will be able to separate us from the love of God in Christ Jesus our Lord. (Rom. 8:35, 38–39)

> The God of peace will soon crush Satan under your feet. The grace of our Lord Jesus Christ be with you. (Rom. 16:20)

> And the devil who had deceived them was thrown into the lake of fire and sulfur where the beast and the false prophet were, and they will be tormented day and night forever and ever. (Rev. 20:10)

To walk with God means to hope in the promises of God. We trust God that heaven is on the way. When you have heaven in view, you don't need a more comfortable and easier "now" to bring you joy. What you need instead is forever to reshape your here and now.[10] Living in light of eternity doesn't remove our pain, but it allows us to have hope in moments of pain.[11]

One of my theology professors, John Hannah, told us to look at all of life as a pointer toward heaven. He encouraged us to look at difficulty and distress in this world as but a taste of the hell that as believers we will never face. And we can consider every delight in life as but a small picture or taste of what our eternity in heaven will be like. Hannah challenged us to remember that in our tough circumstances at work or school, our health issues, or our family problems, our struggles are but a shadow of the eternal damnation that we are free from because of Christ's death on the cross for us. And in every victory and sweet moment in life—graduations, weddings, or quality time together as a family—we realize that they are small pictures of the marvelous eternity we will spend with God because of Christ's death on the cross.

God chose us before the creation of the world, and Christ redeemed us as his brothers and sisters, and he will one day raise us to heaven in glory. "O death, where is your victory? O death, where is your sting?" (1 Cor. 15:55). Friend, what could be better news than this? This land is not our home. As Christians, we are all expatriates, passing through this earth, holding a passport and citizenship to another place. Be encouraged to take the long view in your suffering. This life is a blip on the radar of eternity. It's a small knot in an infinitely long rope. That's why we can say along with the apostle Paul, "We do not lose heart. Though our outer self is wasting away, our inner self is being renewed day by day" (2 Cor. 4:16). Paul's afflictions were quite serious. In many ways they were not slight or momentary. Paul writes later in 2 Corinthians 11 that he has faced imprisonments and countless beatings, often taking him to the point of death. Five times he received the forty lashes minus one from the hands of the Jews. Three times he was beaten with rods, and once he was even stoned. Three times he was shipwrecked, and he spent a day and a night lost at sea.

He faced danger from rivers and robbers and the wilderness and even from his own people. Danger seemed to follow Paul everywhere he went. Sleepless nights and hunger and thirst were constant. And he was burdened for all the churches he planted and for all the pastors he trained and commissioned (2 Cor. 11:23–29). These afflictions lasted his whole life, but he knew they were nothing in comparison with eternity that was coming. A weighty and wonderful eternal glory that was anything but slight and momentary was being prepared for him.[12] He had hope.

How was Paul able to have hope in the midst of these trials? He looked "not to the things that are seen but to the things that are unseen" (2 Cor. 4:18). He knew this life wouldn't last forever. He knew his pain was not the end of the story. Friend, if you are struggling with adversity, sickness, anxiety, fear, or loss of any kind, this too will one day be in the past. What seems so defining and certain now will be done away with. You may feel like your pain is never-ending, but heaven is coming. A time is coming when pain will cease and we will be with our Savior for eternity. This is the real eternal "ever after" that is drawing ever nearer. You may have started reading this chapter ten minutes ago, and are disappointed that the Lord has not returned in the meantime. But we can be assured by this reality: "Salvation is nearer to us now than when we first believed" (Rom. 13:11).

CONCLUSION

Charles Spurgeon once said, "They who dive in the sea of affliction bring up rare pearls."[1] We rarely experience the deepest and most satisfying joys in life while in extended moments of earthly ease. It is in times of trial when we are conformed to the image of Christ. It is in the difficult moments where God shapes us and makes us more like him. It is when walking through trials together that marriages are eventually strengthened, friendships are solidified, and our relationship with God goes deeper. This is why we can count it joy when we face various trials. We can embrace God in our suffering because God is doing a million things for our good and his glory, and we can barely scratch the surface of all he is accomplishing in us in that moment.

I can think of no better way to conclude this book than to tell you about a hero of mine: Glecy Domondon. Glecy was a member of our church for several years. She and her husband, Andy, and their children arrived at Redeemer with about a dozen of their friends in the fall of 2012. They were looking for a church that was preaching the gospel, and they were excited to be a part of our congregation. Throughout the years I grew in my admiration for this sweet couple who trusted God in difficult trials that came their way. The most trying storm was when Glecy began to develop back pain and was diagnosed with aggressive cancer. In the midst of profound pain she trusted God. Her entire family had to move back to the Philippines for her treatment, and I'll never forget the special evening worship gathering where Glecy read a letter to the congregation about what God was doing in her life. It is one of the highlights of my entire pastoral ministry:

> *Good evening. I would like to give an update about my health condition and to share how I am coping with my back pain. I thank God for keeping me and sustaining me over the last six months, and for his goodness over my life and my family. Truly, his grace is sufficient for me, and his strength is made perfect in my weakness. . . . Many of you know that I suffered from chronic pain on my lower back and on my legs. . . . The pain in my spine is irreversible, and what the therapy is doing is just for pain management and to strengthen the core muscles around my spine in order not to worsen my condition.*
>
> *After I came back from the Philippines last January, I had several back pain attacks. The worst attack I had was on March 28. I couldn't walk, I couldn't even stand on my own, and the pain was so severe that my blood pressure rose, resulting in chest pain and breathing difficulty. On that day, Andy brought me to the*

emergency room for treatment but it did not help. I had to admit, it was not easy. I almost gave up, my faith was shaken, but during those moments, I found strength and hope in Christ.

Whom have I in heaven but you? And there is nothing on earth that I desire besides you. My flesh and my heart may fail, but God is the strength of my heart and my portion forever. (Ps. 73:25–26)

For this light momentary affliction is preparing for us an eternal weight of glory beyond all comparison. (2 Cor. 4:17)

And we know that for those who love God all things work together for good, for those who are called according to his purpose. (Rom. 8:28)

With all that truth flooding in my mind, I was encouraged and reminded that God is sovereign and he is in control of everything, even in my suffering. I know he is good and he does all things according to his purpose. And the joy I have found is in the grace of God manifested in the death and resurrection of our Lord and Savior Jesus Christ, who suffered so much for me and for his people. Isaiah writes: "Surely he has borne our griefs and carried our sorrows; yet we esteemed him stricken, smitten by God, and afflicted. But he was wounded for our transgressions; he was crushed for our iniquities; upon him was the chastisement that

> *brought us peace, and with his stripes we are healed" (Isa. 53:4–5).*
>
> *Every day, I have learned to trust God for His grace: "The steadfast love of the LORD never ceases; his mercies never come to an end; they are new every morning; great is your faithfulness" (Lam. 3:22–23).*
>
> *Thank God for his healing grace. Thank you for your prayers and encouragements.*

This sweet testimony of a child of God fighting for joy makes my heart soar. Glecy Domondon fought for faith in life-threatening trials because she knew her life was bound up in Jesus. Her testimony to our church is exactly what this book has been about. How do we embrace God in the midst of our trials? How do we look to him when we feel like we're drowning in despair? We remember the Lord. We remember what he has done for us. We look to God and every spiritual blessing in the heavenly places that he has given us in Christ. We choose to live in the privilege of our adoption and the comfort that we are known by God. We glory in our Redeemer who died on the cross to save us from our sins. We rest in his finished work and know that our God is in control over everything. He is our refuge, and he will never leave us. He will keep us to the end, and there will be a day when all suffering will cease and we will be face-to-face with Jesus for eternity.

It was an incredibly sad moment when I got the message that Glecy had passed away in the Philippines. We lost an amazing woman that day. But we will get her back in the new creation. I was glad to see her husband, Andy, recently when he visited our church. We were able to give each other a hug and pray together and remember his wife, a sweet sister who trusted God in her fiery trial. Through tears, Andy recounted his wife's strength even in weakness. She was able to embrace God and trust him because even in her darkest times, she knew that her Savior reigned. I pray God gives you the strength to do the same.

Appendix:

RECOMMENDED RESOURCES

Chapter 1: Look to the Savior in the Storm

Spiritual Depression: Its Causes and Its Cure by D. Martyn Lloyd-Jones. Lloyd-Jones challenges us to stop listening to ourselves and instead talk to ourselves. Rather than listen to lies, we must inject the truth of the gospel into our minds and hearts each day. In a sense, Lloyd-Jones says that all of us are preachers. We may not preach from a pulpit, but we must preach to ourselves—every day.

How Long, O Lord?: Reflections on Suffering and Evil by D. A. Carson. This work is longer and a bit more technical than some of Carson's other writings, but the last chapters are especially devotional as he considers both the mystery and comfort of Providence. He concludes with helpful pastoral reflections.

Evangelism and the Sovereignty of God by J. I. Packer. While the title indicates that this is a book on evangelism (and it is), it is also one of the best books I have read on the sovereignty of God. God holds the whole world in his hands, and this informs everything we do.

Chapter 2: He Is Our Refuge

A Grief Observed by C. S. Lewis. After his wife's tragic death, Lewis penned this honest work as he fought for faith in the midst of his tremendous loss. It's his account of being on the verge of drowning and yet gradually coming to understand that God is with him.

The Glories of God's Love: A Gospel Primer for Christians by Milton Vincent. This short book filled with gospel truth applied to every area of life challenged me to look at trials as an opportunity for God to do an amazing work in and through people.

Note to Self: The Discipline of Preaching to Yourself by Joe Thorn. This book is full of hope-filled reminders of what God has done in our lives.

Chapter 3: The Ultimate Rescue Mission

Christ Our Life by Michael Reeves. An excellent book on Christ before the creation, Christ in the incarnation, the crucifixion, our life in Christ, and the truth that he will return to usher in eternity.

The First Days of Jesus: The Story of the Incarnation by Andreas J. Köstenberger and Alexander Stewart. This book leads the reader step-by-step through the birth narratives in the Gospels in a soul-stirring way. It looks at Jesus as the virgin-born Messiah, the light of the nations, and the incarnate Word.

Chapter 4: The Greatest Exchange in All of History

Gospel for Real Life: Turn to the Liberating Power of the Cross . . . Every Day by Jerry Bridges. Bridges writes about different facets of the gospel and reminds us that the gospel is something we need every single day.

Redemption Accomplished and Applied by John Murray. I know of no better book on the atonement and the application of it in our lives.

In My Place Condemned He Stood: Celebrating the Glory of the Atonement by J. I. Packer and Mark Dever. This book includes a chapter on the heart of the gospel and what the cross achieved. Certainly worth the price of the book is Packer's introduction to John Owen's *The Death of Death in the Death of Christ*.

It Is Well: Expositions on Substitutionary Atonement by Mark Dever and Michael Lawrence. An excellent series of expository sermons on various aspects of the death of Christ.

Chapter 5: Jesus is Raised

Raised with Christ: How the Resurrection Changes Everything by Adrian Warnock. Warnock shows that the resurrection is not just a truth that confirms the atonement of Christ but one that transforms us and leads us to a revival of prayer and a renewed relationship with the risen Jesus.

The Final Days of Jesus: The Most Important Week of the Most Important Person Who Ever Lived by Andreas J. Köstenberger and Justin Taylor. This book gives an overview of the last week of Christ's life including his entrance into Jerusalem, the plot against Jesus, and his final discourse, arrest, death on the cross, burial, and resurrection. The last section detailing the empty tomb and aftermath is concise and especially helpful in considering the truth and reality of the resurrection.

Chapter 6: Look, I Am Your Father

Adopted for Life: The Priority of Adoption for Christian Families and Churches by Russell Moore. This book was the driving force in my life to start thinking about the gospel imagery of adoption. Moore examines the Scriptures and shows how as Christians we have been adopted by God and are a part of his family.

Heirs with Christ: The Puritans on Adoption by Joel Beeke. This little book shows how the Puritans talked about adoption and its transforming power and comfort for God's children.

Chapter 7: He Really Knows Every Hair on Your Head

Knowing God by J. I. Packer. Chapter 3 is a helpful meditation on how our great God actually knows *us*. Our names are graven on his hands.

The Attributes of God by Arthur Pink. The sections on the knowledge of God and the love of God are helpful.

Chapter 8: Our Pain Has a Glorious Purpose

The Holiness of God by R. C. Sproul. This is a classic work on the perfection of God. He is holy, we must be at peace with this holy God, and our lives must change and continue to become more and more like him.

Night of Weeping: When God's Children Suffer by Horatius Bonar. In this lesser-known work, Bonar shows us that God has many purposes in our suffering.

The Hole in Our Holiness: Filling the Gap between Gospel Passion and the Pursuit of Godliness by Kevin DeYoung. DeYoung exhorts the Christian that the pursuit of sanctification is a fight. We must not only believe the gospel—we must live in light of it, which includes both remembering it and fighting sin with all of our energy and effort.

Chapter 9: Weakness Is Always the Way

Weakness Is the Way: Life with Christ Our Strength by J. I. Packer. God uses the weak in extraordinary ways to show the world that it's Christ who gets the glory. Packer shows this glorious truth by briefly sharing his story and then looking at the Scriptures to show that this has always been God's plan.

The Bruised Reed by Richard Sibbes. Sibbes focuses more on our weakness and misery that come as a result of sin, but the point is that when we are brought to the end of ourselves, we have no alternative than to go to Christ for help. We will face trials and we may feel bruised, but God will not forever break us.

Chapter 10: You Are a Part of Christ's Body

Life Together by Dietrich Bonhoeffer. This is the best book on community I have ever read. It is a reminder to me not to retreat away from others in my trials. The church is a blessing to the hurting, and we should do whatever we can to be with the bride of Christ.

Compelling Community: Where God's Power Makes a Church Attractive by Mark Dever and Jamie Dunlop. This book talks about how the power of the gospel brings God's people together in ways that transcend all boundaries.

Why Bother with Church: And Other Questions about Why You Need It and Why It Needs You by Sam Allberry. This is an excellent book that will encourage weary hearts with the truth that the church needs the broken and the hurting to join in (along with all others) to truly be Christ's glorious body here on earth.

Chapter 11: Christ Will Hold You Fast

Run to Win the Prize: Perseverance in the New Testament by Thomas R. Schreiner. This is a technical primer on perseverance as seen throughout Scripture. The chapter on how persevering faith is not perfection is an encouragement.

Chapter 12: Extreme Makeover

Future Grace: The Purifying Power of the Promises of God by John Piper. I found the last chapters on the future grace of suffering, the future grace of dying, and the rebirth of creation helpful as I considered suffering and eternity.

Chapter 13: Heaven Is for Real

Forever: Why You Can't Live Without It by Paul David Tripp. This is one of the most hope-filled books Tripp has written. The reality of forever does not just come after we die, but it should affect our every day. The thought of forever should transform our relationships, our parenting, our jobs, and our relationship with God. Forever should change our everything.

SCRIPTURE INDEX

NOTES

Introduction

1 I first wrote about my story of suffering in "Dealing Hope in the Darkest of Nights," Desiring God website, September 5, 2016, https://www.desiringgod.org/articles/dealing-hope-in-the-darkest-of-nights

2 Darrel W. Amundsen, "The Anguish and Agonies of Charles Spurgeon," *Christian History*, no. 29 (1991): 24.

3 People debate the content of Spurgeon's exact quote. This quote has been attributed to Spurgeon for decades, and it is possible that he said it at some point, perhaps even out of the pulpit. However, Christian George, a Spurgeon scholar, cites a slightly different quote, which is the closest thing we can find in an official Spurgeon sermon: "The wave of temptation may even wash you higher up upon the Rock of ages, so that you cling to it with a firmer grip than you have ever done before, and so again where sin abounds, grace will much more abound." Christian George, "6 Things Spurgeon Didn't Say," The Spurgeon Center, https://www.spurgeon.org/resource-library/blog-entries/6-things-spurgeon-didnt-say/

4 Milton Vincent, *The Glories of God's Love: A Gospel Primer for Christians* (Leyland, UK: 10Publishing, 2015), 24.

5 R.E.M, "Everybody Hurts," 1992.

6 Tim Keller, *Walking with God through Pain and Suffering* (New York: Dutton, 2013), 3.

Chapter 1: Look to the Savior in the Storm

1 Don and Susie Van Ryn, Newell Colleen, and Whitney Cerak, *Mistaken Identity: Two Families, One Survivor, Unwavering Hope* (Brentwood, TN: Howard Books, 2009).

2 The description of the gale fits that of the well-known easterly wind known as the *Sharkia* (Arabic, "shark"), which usually starts in early evening and is good cause for apprehension among fishermen. J. R. Edwards, *The Gospel According to Mark,* The Pillar New Testament Commentary (Grand Rapids, MI: Eerdmans, 2002), 197.

3 J. R. Edwards, *The Gospel According to Mark,* The Pillar New Testament Commentary (Grand Rapids, MI: Eerdmans, 2002), 198.

4 Ibid.

5 Ibid.

6 I heard Paul David Tripp say something similar to this in a sermon on Mark 6.

Chapter 2: He Is Our Refuge

1 D. A. Carson, *How Long, O Lord?* (Grand Rapids, MI: Baker Academic, 1990), 63.

2 Charles Spurgeon, *The Treasury of David,* vol. 1 (Peabody, MA: Hendrickson, 1988), 341.

3 J. M. Boice, *Psalms 42–106: An Expositional Commentary* (Grand Rapids, MI: Baker, 2005), 389.

Chapter 3: The Ultimate Rescue Mission

1 D. A. Carson, *The God Who Is There* (Grand Rapids, MI: Baker, 2010), 14–15.

2 Michael Reeves, *Christ Our Life* (Milton Keynes, UK: Paternoster Press, 2013), 34.

Chapter 4: The Greatest Exchange in All of History

1 Mark Galli, "Let Kelly Gissendaner Live," *CT* online, March 3, 2015, https://www.christianitytoday.com/ct/2015/march-web-only/let-kelly-gissendaner-live.html

2 David Cook, "Cook: The Life, Death, and Ressurrection of Kelly Gissendaner," *Times Free Press* online, March 1, 2015, https://www.timesfreepress.com/news/2015/mar/01/life-death-and-resurrectikelly-gissendaner/

3 I heard Tim Keller paint a wonderful picture of this scene in a sermon on this text. Timothy J. Keller, "Mark 15:1–15, King's Cross: The Gospel of Mark, Part 2: The Journey to the Cross" (New York: Redeemer Presbyterian Church, March 11, 2007).

4 Ibid.

5 Ibid.

6 Timothy S. Lane and Paul David Tripp, *How People Change* (Greensboro, NC: New Growth Press, 2006), 1–15.

7 D. Martyn Lloyd-Jones, *Spiritual Depression: Its Causes and Cure* (Grand Rapids, MI: Eerdmans, 1965), 20–21.

8 Rhonda Cook, "She Sang Amazing Grace Then the Drugs Took Hold and She Stuttered into Silence," *DailyMail.com*, Sept. 30, 2015, https://www.dailymail.co.uk/news/article-3255523/She-sang-Amazing-Grace-drugs-took-hold-stuttered-silence-state-Georgia-executes-woman-70-years-chilling-dispatch-inside-chamber.html

9 Rachel Lynn Aldrich, "Georgia Death Row Inmate Shows 'Concrete Fruit of Redemption'," *World*, March 3, 2015, https://wng.org/sift/georgia-death-row-inmate-shows-concrete-fruit-of-redemption-1618205538

Chapter 5: Jesus is Raised

1 This language of the hope of the resurrection is often attributed to the late church historian Jaroslav Pelikan.

2 Joni Eareckson Tada, *Heaven: Your Real Home* (Grand Rapids, MI: Zondervan, 2012), 64–65.

Chapter 6: Look, I Am Your Father

1 John Murray, *Redemption Accomplished and Applied* (Grand Rapids, MI: Eerdmans, 1955), 132.

2 Ibid., 134.

3 D. Martyn Lloyd-Jones, *The Sons of God: Exposition of Chapter 8:5–17* (Edinburgh, Scotland: Banner of Truth, 1974), 280.

4 Philip Graham Ryken, *Galatians,* Reformed Expository Commentary (Phillipsburg, NJ: P&R, 2005), 167.

5 Timothy Keller, *Galatians for You* (Surrey, UK: The Good Book Company, 2013), 100.

6 Ryken, Galatians, 167.

7 Ibid.

8 D. A. Carson, "Matthew," in *The Expositor's Bible Commentary*, ed. Frank E. Gaebelein, vol. 8, *Matthew, Mark, Luke* (Grand Rapids, MI: Zondervan, 1984), 166.

9 Ibid.

10 Horatius Bonar, *Night of Weeping: When God's Children's Suffer* (Ross-shire, UK: Christian Focus, 1999), 16.

Chapter 7: He Really Knows Every Hair on Your Head

1 BBC, "Tourist Walks Off Australia Pier While Checking Facebook," December 19, 2013, https://www.bbc.com/news/world-asia-25426263

2 Blaise Pascal, *Pensees* (New York: Penguin, 1966), 75.

3 John Piper, *Think: The Life of the Mind and the Love of God* (Wheaton, IL: Crossway, 2011), 160–61.

4 J. I. Packer, *Knowing God* (Downers Grove, IL: InterVarsity Press, 1993), 41–42.

5 Brian Rosner, "Known by God: The Meaning and Value of a Neglected Biblical Concept," *Tyndale Bulletin* 59, no. 2 (2008): 207–8.

6 Richard Baxter, *The Practical Works of Rev. Richard Baxter*, vol. 15 (London: James Duncan, 1830), 285.

7 Brian Rosner, "Known by God," Ridley College website, June 11, 2015, https://www.ridley.edu.au/resource/known-by-god-2/

Chapter 8: Our Pain Has a Glorious Purpose

1 This material on the vine and pruning was taught me by J. Dwight Pentecost during my time at seminary in a course on the Upper Room Discourse.

2 D. A. Carson, *How Long, O Lord?* (Grand Rapids, MI: Baker Academic, 1990), 72.

3 For a practical treatment on the subject of idolatry, please see chapter 3 of Timothy Keller's excellent study, *Gospel in Life* (Grand Rapids: Zondervan, 2010). These questions were adapted from pages 41–42.

4 David Powlison and Paul David Tripp, *Changing Hearts, Changing Lives* (Greensboro, NC: New Growth Press, 2006), DVD.

5 Charles Spurgeon, *Treasuring of David* (Peabody, MA: Hendrickson, 1990), 359.

6 D. A. Carson, *For the Love of God : A Daily Companion for Discovering the Riches of God's Word,* vol. 2 (Wheaton, IL: Crossway, 1998), 25.

7 Kevin DeYoung, *The Hole in Our Holiness* (Wheaton, IL: Crossway, 2012), 19.

Chapter 9: Weakness Is Always the Way

1 I first read about *Kintsugi* from a newsletter sent out by Community Arts Tokyo, which pointed out this very truth about weakness (January 2016).

2 For an extraordinary treatment of this concept please see J. I. Packer's book by the same title: *Weakness Is the Way* (Wheaton, IL: Crossway, 2013).

3 Packer, *Weakness Is the Way*, 49.

4 Paul Barnett, *The Message of 2 Corinthians: Power in Weakness* in The Bible Speaks Today (Downers Grove, IL: InterVarsity Press, 1988), 90.

5 Packer, *Weakness Is the Way*, 22.

6 Alister McGrath, *J. I. Packer: A Biography* (Grand Rapids, MI: Baker, 1997), 6.

Chapter 10: You Are a Part of Christ's Body

1 Leon Morris, *1 Corinthians: An Introduction and Commentary*, vol. 7 (Downers Grove, IL: InterVarsity Press, 1985), 169.

2 Ibid., 170.

3 Sam Allberry, *Why Bother with Church? And Other Questions about Why You Need It and It Needs You* (Epsom, UK: The Good Book Company, 2016), 34–35.

4 Morris, *1 Corinthians*, 170–71.

5 Ibid.

6 I once heard my friend Albert Tate share a similar illustration about how the show *Matlock* related to corporate worship.

7 Thanks to Tim Keller for the initial idea behind this illustration.

Chapter 11: Christ Will Hold You Fast

1 R. C. Sproul, *What Is Reformed Theology?* (Grand Rapids, MI: Baker, 1997), 202.

2 Ibid., 201.

3 T. R. Schreiner, *1, 2 Peter, Jude* in The New American Commentary, vol. 37 (Nashville: Broadman & Holman, 2003), 64.

4 Sproul, *What Is Reformed Theology?*, 210.

5 Ibid., 204.

6 Milton Vincent, *The Glories of God's Love: A Gospel Primer for Christians* (Leyland, UK: 10Publishing, 2015), 16.

7 Thomas R. Schreiner, *Run to Win the Prize* (Wheaton, IL: Crossway, 2010), 18–19.

8 Timothy Keller, *The Reason for God* (New York: Dutton, 2008), 234.

Chapter 12: Extreme Makeover

1 J. I. Packer, *Weakness Is the Way* (Wheaton, IL: Crossway, 2013), 108.

2 Ibid., 107.

3 Richard R. Melick, *Philippians, Colossians, Philemon* in The New American Commentary, vol. 32 (Nashville: Broadman & Holman, 1991), 144.

4 J. A. Motyer, *The Message of Philippians*, The Bible Speaks Today (Downers Grove, IL: InterVarsity Press, 1984), 195.

5 Ibid.

6 Leon Morris, *1 Corinthians: An Introduction and Commentary, Vol. 7* (Downers Grove, IL: InterVarsity Press, 1985), 213.

7 Ibid.

8 Packer, *Weakness Is the Way*, 114.

9 John Piper, *Future Grace* (Sisters, OR: Multnomah, 1995), 358–59.

10 Ibid., 359.

11 Ibid., 360.

Chapter 13: Heaven Is for Real

1 Tim Challies, "Heaven Tourism," *Challies* (blog), June 18, 2012, https://www.challies.com/articles/heaven-tourism/

2 Bill Chappell, *Boy Says He Didn't Go to Heaven*, NPR website, January 15, 2015, https://www.npr.org/sections/thetwo-way/2015/01/15/377589757/boy-says-he-didn-t-go-to-heaven-publisher-says-it-will-pull-book

3 G. K. Beale, *The Book of Revelation: A Commentary on the Greek Text* (Grand Rapids, MI: Eerdmans, 1999), 1040.

4 G. K. Beale and David H. Campbell, *Revelation: A Shorter Commentary* (Grand Rapids, MI: Eerdmans, 2015), 464.

5 Beale, *Revelation*, 1115–116.

6 Ibid.

7 Leon Morris, *Revelation: An Introduction and Commentary*, vol. 20 (Downers Grove, IL: InterVarsity Press, 1987), 244.

8 Beale, *Revelation*, 1114.

9 Steve Brown, *What Was I Thinking?: Things I've Learned Since I Knew It All* (New York: Howard, 2006), 90.

10 Paul David Tripp, *Forever: Why You Can't Live without It* (Grand Rapids, MI: Zondervan, 2011), 36.

11 Ibid., 73.

12 C. G. Kruse, *2 Corinthians: An Introduction and Commentary*, vol. 8 (Downers Grove, IL: InterVarsity Press, 1987), 110.

Conclusion

1 Charles H. Spurgeon, *Spurgeon on Prayer* (Alachua, FL: Bridge Logos, 2009), 294.